Smart Talk

MELISSA VELA-WILLIAMSON, APR, CDP

Smart Talk

Public Relations Essentials
All Pros Should Know

LIONCREST
PUBLISHING

Smart Talk

Public Relations Essentials All Pros Should Know

ISBN 978-1-5445-3248-6 Hardcover
      978-1-5445-3247-9 Paperback
      978-1-5445-3249-3 Ebook

To God

who called me to write this book

and all who honor me

by reading it.

Contents

Introduction. *1*

CHAPTER 1 9
What PR *Really* Is

CHAPTER 2 . . . .*31*
Start Smart with PR Etiquette

CHAPTER 3 . . . .*53*
Media Relations Do's and Don'ts

CHAPTER 4 . . . .*85*
Planning Like a Pro

CHAPTER 5 . . . . *117*
The Relationships You Need to Be Successful

CHAPTER 6 . . . . *141*
Use Tailoring to Serve Multicultural Needs

CHAPTER 7 . . . . *165*

Understanding Integrated Marketing Communication

CHAPTER 8 . . . . *189*

Building Your PR Toolkit

CHAPTER 9 . . . . *211*

Think Like a Pro

CHAPTER 10 . . . . *225*

Act Like a Pro

Conclusion *247*

Acknowledgments *253*

Introduction

HAVE YOU EVER BEEN A PART OF A CONVERSATION THAT was going nowhere? Or had words coming at you, but they weren't lining up in a way that made sense? For some people, listening to an academic lecture or presentation filled with industry jargon can feel like that type of blathering. Or, you may know the feeling from having spoken with a passive-aggressive person who just can't (or won't) say the uncomfortable or hard thing they need to say.

As a public relations (PR) professional, I hate wasting time trying to decode communication like that. Life is much too noisy, and work is much too fast-paced not to get to the point. Personally, I skim over unnecessarily detailed paragraphs in books, fast forward through commercials, and may tune out people who don't communicate in a clear, impactful way. Professionally, I want to have deep conversations that uncover helpful truths, clarify confusing concepts, and allow me to connect with others. I call this **smart talk**—real, honest, helpful conversations with an intelligent exchange of information and stories. Smart talk isn't always comfortable, but neither is personal growth. Our growth as professionals is more probable when we don't beat around the bush. Working in PR can be full of enough unpredictable moments as it is.

About two years into my PR career, I worked at a nonprofit. On behalf of the organization, I would coordinate media interviews, advertising, and partnerships with a radio station marketing executive named Scott. He was an influential and unconventional person. He decided which radio station public service announcements, community affair show interviews, and partnerships happened. During our initial meeting, he showed me around his office. He pointed out cool celebrity photos, offered me a snack, and then we sat down for our chat. Suddenly, he grabbed a nearby neon-yellow hand towel and threw it onto his desk. He looked at me with a smirk.

"What's that?" I asked.

He picked it up and let me read it.

"Bullshit…" I read aloud. "Why do you have a bullshit towel?"

"It's a bullshit *flag*," he corrected me. "I throw it on the table during meetings whenever someone is bullshitting me."

You'd better believe I wasn't prepared for *that* as a new PR pro.

Luckily, I wasn't BS-ing him then, and I won't BS you now. This book is full of smart talk about PR. I'm sharing honest, insightful, and sometimes cringeworthy stories from my two decades in the trenches. The information and career lessons are for people like you—aspiring PR professionals who want to know the essentials of the practice so you can avoid the pitfalls. I'm offering you authentic, helpful, and encouraging insights into the most important parts of PR today. You won't need to throw a flag on anything you read here!

I have grown immensely since my wobbly first years as an excited but ill-equipped PR coordinator. Nearly 20 years later, I am an internationally recognized and award-winning PR business owner who has worked in or with just about every sector of PR possible. I've worked as an employee at a boutique Hispanic-focused PR agency, for a nonprofit, for a large corporation, and at a large, full-service PR agency. I've targeted the general market audience as well as niche multicultural audiences in a variety of PR, marketing, advertising, community relations, and social media campaigns. I also have the rare experience of working in employee communications and in diversity, equity, and inclusion (DEI). That combination gives me confidence in working through a variety of communication challenges and with a variety of people.

Since 2015, I have served clients as the founder of my own national, award-winning boutique firm, MVW Communications. In my business, I can work directly as a consultant with a client or as an account director with an assembled team of communication experts. We tailor our approach and team size depending on each client's communication challenge and budget. My own breadth and depth of communication experience inspires our 360-degree communication perspective, but my expertise, accreditation, and heart are in PR.

During my career, I have worked with over 90 brands, such as Kampgrounds of America, H-E-B, Alamo Colleges District, Meals on Wheels San Antonio, Big Brothers Big Sisters, and Girl Scouts of Southwest Texas. I never imagined I'd be sought after for advice, but I feel called to give it. I am proud to share best practices from my experiences as a thought leader in the field. I write for PR pros across the nation as a Public Relations Society of America columnist—the first to ever focus on the Hispanic and Latino market. I educate organizations and aspiring PR pros as a trainer and a professional speaker. I enjoy sharing my ideas with trade journalists at PRNEWS, and I have even represented the United States on an international panel of the Public Relations and Communications Association (PRCA Americas)—the world's largest professional PR body. That's what's so amazing about this work: you never know where you could end up! My passion for elevating the industry has inspired me to reach out to others and to serve at a higher capacity to make places for pros of color. It also emboldened me to launch my podcast, *Smart Talk Series.* I love PR so much that I created an online merchandise shop called PR Pro Gear where pros can buy mugs and shirts about it! I found my own way into PR, but it was a rough road. Now, I want to invite others like me who lacked connections, education, or guidance onto a smoother path forward into the field.

This book is a scalable way for me to share answers to questions I frequently receive from aspiring pros. More importantly, this is where I can encourage you to join the PR club. We need diverse pros in this industry more than ever. It's a more multiracial and multicultural world each day, and our PR workforce should reflect that.

However, the lack of institutions offering PR as an undergraduate major, the lack of paid internship options, and the lack of current representation in the field can discourage students from diverse backgrounds from entering. Without some bridge from the classroom to the career, college graduates' lack of awareness of PR, misunderstanding of what the profession entails, and lack of real-world experience prevents them from getting on the PR career track.

Similarly, journalists who transition into PR to get a more manageable schedule, earn higher pay, or increase their advancement opportunities soon realize there's much more to PR than just media relations. They often struggle to learn the many other disciplines of the job without embarrassing themselves or being labeled as inadequate once in. A lack of comprehensive PR career training can increase the likelihood of mistakes and perpetuate misunderstandings about the field.

Students who are curious about PR or officially studying it as a major can benefit from the advice in these pages. It doesn't matter how many courses you took or didn't take—this is your guidebook. No textbook written by academics can replace the lessons from those who actually work in the industry. This book is also for journalists who are considering changing careers and moving into PR. And this is for journalists who are already working in PR and have realized they didn't know how broad the profession was. Marketers who do PR activities and need more guidance are also welcome.

Anyone who reads this book will learn everything I didn't know when I started in PR. I'm offering you the mentoring moments you may need and the advice I wish I'd had when starting out. There are nuances in the work that it takes decades to learn. I'll share those with you, along with insights that will make new(er) pros more successful. As you read this book, you'll learn ways to be more marketable, earn more media coverage, and be more prepared for crisis communication issues. More importantly, I'll share PR principles and methods that will allow you to leapfrog ahead and avoid mistakes.

Throughout the book, you'll learn how your own lived experiences and cultural practices can help you do well as a PR professional. You can consider if you're a "fit" based on the work involved in PR, not by your background. People from diverse or even *adverse* backgrounds are uniquely suited to thrive in PR.

This book will not include PR history or theory. This writing is a holistic look at the most important aspects of the field you must know and embrace to become a strong candidate or professional. Beyond the fundamentals, I've added insights into where the PR field is going and why I think integration with other fields will lead to a more progressive, inclusive practice. Throughout the book, I'll introduce bold terms you should know and define them so that we're speaking about the same things in the same way. As you read, highlight helpful lines, fold page corners, and mark this book up. Do whatever works to help you absorb the lessons and apply them right away.

Ultimately, this book is for anyone who wants to learn the essentials of succeeding in PR. My lived experience as a second-generation Hispanic American, a first-generation university graduate and an unsuspecting pioneer in many other ways will be woven throughout the advice shared. Guest voices from diverse professionals I admire are included so that different perspectives can be considered. Learn from their advice in each chapter's "Pass the Mic" closing thought.

Statistically, I'm not supposed to be writing this book. I represent part of only 10.5% of Hispanics/Latinos in the US who report working in PR, according to the 2019 Census. Latino authors make up only 7.2% of the publishing industry. But here I am! A strong work ethic, willingness to learn, and curious nature can take you far. I started as a PR coordinator with little formal academic PR knowledge, no portfolio of experience, and no friends in the field. Now I'm an accredited and award-winning

PR strategist who runs her own agency, hosts a podcast, and writes for the leading PR association in the nation. What I have achieved in this profession was not passed down through generations of family experience or through a preestablished network. I've learned to ask for help, do the most with what I have, and creatively solve problems. Now, I feel equipped to invest in supporting the diversification and advancement of this field. That is my new calling, and I hope what I share inspires you to pay it forward too.

For many of us, we don't know someone like us who works in PR. Don't let that stop you from seeing yourself as a fit for this industry. Let me be your trusted guide and confirm that *you* can do well in PR. This book is my written invitation for you to join in. Come with me on this journey. We are proud to have you as part of the club. Read on for the essential information you need to get started.

CHAPTER 1

~

What PR *Really* Is

EVERY YEAR, I SPEAK WITH AMBITIOUS STUDENTS WHO know what they'd like to do after college. They're studying for their field of choice, lining up internships, and they seem on a smooth path forward. That wasn't my story.

When I was in high school, I knew I *should* go to college to find a good career, but I wasn't sure *what* that career would be. I was a late bloomer academically and weighed over 200 pounds on a 5' 1" frame as a high school freshman. Luckily, one teacher, Ms. Ash, saw a gift in my writing during eighth grade. She registered me for my first honors class—ninth grade English Honors. Inviting me onto the honors track changed everything. Kids in honors classes at my Title I high school were on a different level. They were intelligent, kinder, and competitive about their grades. Being judged on my achievements instead of my appearance was easier. All my potential became apparent once I was paired with higher-caliber students. That first semester of high school, I walked into my counselor's office and demanded all my classes be changed to honors. Leveling up my network, advocating for myself, and embracing learning altered the direction of my future.

By graduation, all my A's, marching band medals, and achievements started losing value. It was time to go to college and begin adulting. I was too intimidated to try a large university, so I followed some friends to a small, but expensive, private university. Finding my way into PR happened almost by accident.

As a college student, I struggled to find a career path. I wanted to be a veterinarian, but I dropped that major once I experienced my first long lab class. Changing to an English/Communication Arts major was a better fit. But what could I do with that?

I knew I excelled at creative writing and had worked summer jobs in photography. Still, being a poet or a photographer wasn't a stable career, and I had student loans piling up. I spent many days at Career Services, reading about career options and trying to figure out what to do.

Many communication students have heard of advertising and would love to work in advertising jobs. Not as many seem aware of PR, though. Few universities have a PR major or advanced classes on the subject. In fact, the National Center for Education Statistics listed only 10 colleges with a PR program! While they may have missed a few, you get the picture. Perhaps the lack of a defined major is because so many academics and pros lump marketing and PR together. Public relations can be seen as a marketing activity. The areas are different, though—both in purpose and in practice. Whatever the reason, students, especially those at minority-serving institutions or smaller colleges, often lack exposure to PR as a career option. Fewer learn how to adequately prepare for work in the field. That was exactly my experience as an undergraduate. Luckily, another student shared her internship experience with me, and that sparked my interest.

During my senior year in college, students in our major were asked to research a profession we wanted to work in and present it to the class. I still wasn't sure what type of career would be right for me. I had completed a marketing internship and could do that, but I wasn't satisfied by promotions. Research for this capstone presentation led me to learn about becoming an advertising copywriter, so I presented on that. Working at a big advertising firm sounded cool but unlikely.

My classmate Kate gave a presentation about the PR field and how much she had enjoyed her PR internship. The way she described working with a rehab system that empowered people with disabilities to water ski using adaptive equipment sounded so purposeful. She was able to work with the skiers, learn their backstories, and pitch a story idea to a local reporter. She showed us the printed newspaper story along with a photo of a man without legs zipping happily across a lake. I got the goose bumps I had been looking for! Through PR, she was helping others,

SMART TALK

telling untold stories, and managing elements of marketing that I thought were fun. It sounded heart-based, people-focused, and diverse enough to fit my multipassionate spirit. Sold! A lot of hustle, a little luck, and a friend's referral helped me find my first shot at working in the field (you'll learn more about how I got my start in Chapter 2).

DEFINING PUBLIC RELATIONS TODAY

I've invested almost two decades of my life working in PR. There are many misconceptions about PR, so I'll clear them up for you. To get on the same page, let's define PR from a workplace perspective.

According to the Public Relations Society of America (PRSA), the nation's leading PR professional trade organization, **PR** is "a strategic communication process that builds mutually beneficial relationships between organizations and their publics."

Public relations is not about making a quick sale today. It's about building relationships with your customers for the long haul so that through good and bad, they'll look to your organization for products or services, to volunteer with, or to donate money to.

This work consists of influencing, engaging, and managing relationships with key **stakeholders:** people who matter to your organization. We communicate across media types (or mediums) to shape and frame the perception of the organization. PR pros earn those stakeholder relationships like they earn media coverage. What is earned usually cannot be paid for. Rather, you *earn* relationships or media coverage through merit and not by paying to guarantee your outcome like you can with advertising efforts.

In comparison, **marketing** is "the activity, set of institutions, and processes for creating, communicating, delivering, and exchanging offerings that have value for customers, clients, partners, and society at large," according to the American Marketing Association. Marketing is about an exchange—where a relationship is based on a transaction. Marketers create a desire in consumers so that their organization can exchange the right goods or services for money or support. Creating that consumer demand is fundamental to marketing. Marketing and PR should work together, and the best of PR professionals will integrate the two areas to develop a cohesive campaign. We'll dive deeper into that area, **integrated marketing communication,** in Chapter 7.

Many people think PR pros only do **media relations** or work with journalists to get their clients' or organizations' stories in the news. Many of us do **publicity** work—earning unpaid positive media (a.k.a. news) coverage in outlets like newspapers, radio, TV, magazines, online publications, or podcasts. But that's only *one* aspect of the work pros do. According to PRSA, there are 13 major disciplines undertaken by PR pros:

1. Brand journalism/content creation
2. Corporate communications
3. Crisis communications
4. Event planning and management
5. Executive communications
6. Governmental relations/public affairs
7. Internal/employee communications
8. Marketing communications
9. Media relations and social media influencer relations
10. Multimedia production
11. Reputation management
12. Social media strategy and management
13. Speechwriting and ghostwriting

This list doesn't cover everything, but it shows many specialized focus areas within PR. This often surprises people who don't work in the field.

FOCUS YOUR PR POINT OF VIEW

In my career, I've worked in every major sector of PR—a Hispanic boutique agency, a nonprofit, a corporation, and the largest full-service communication agency in South Texas. No matter my role, I always saw each challenge from a PR point of view (POV). Before I started my job at Big Brothers Big Sisters, I asked if they would change my title from Recruiting and Marketing Coordinator to Recruiting and Public Relations Coordinator. Why would I do that? Because I knew the relationships I could establish and the real-life stories I could tell through PR would be far more valuable to recruiting volunteers than any marketing promotion or advertising campaign would be. I wanted to be seen as someone who was people-focused. My hunch was right; the stories I told about everyday people who were Big Brother and Big Sister mentors inspired more volunteer interest than any piece of marketing collateral we created. It was because of the relationships I made with those mentors that they were willing to do interviews, be in photoshoots, and support the organization in extraordinary ways. I knew by then that words matter and that my title would be part of my job identity. When you say you're in marketing, people often think more about being *sold to* rather than *related to*.

No matter what type of communication role or work you do, you can do it from a PR POV. Think about your work like a PR pro. Will what you're doing produce long-term results? Will it create beneficial relationships? Is it ethically sound, and are you doing more good than harm? That framework can shape anything you communicate: from social media campaigns; to how you direct an advertising commercial; to how you write copy for a marketing brochure; and more.

Get ready to ask lots of "why" questions and to challenge decisions at all levels of management because of your PR POV.

It's better for us to find the mistakes or issues before the public does! PR people are not "yes people." We should be advisers, conduct research, make plans inspired by facts, and change or adapt those plans as needed. Our role is to try to prevent issues and put out small fires before they burn the place down. Unfortunately, like insurance policies, people don't always comprehend the value our coverage provides.

COMPETENCIES OF A PRO

There are competencies you need to do well in PR. First, it helps if you have a good understanding of ethics, a deep understanding of whom your organization serves, a strong writing ability, and the ability to practice discernment. You'll also want to be an agile problem-solver and a solid editor. You should be comfortable selling an idea, be willing to take rejection, and show care for humanity. Here's a list of some of the roles PR pros may have to play:

- Advisers/counselors
- Brand managers
- Community organizers
- Communication planners
- Content creators or managers
- Event planners
- Researchers

- Project managers
- Publicists
- Spokespeople
- Writers
- And so much more

We're like the Swiss Army knives of communicators but with big hearts, thick skins, and whistle-blowing responsibilities. Being good at the fundamentals of PR will help across all the types of tasks you'll do.

PR CAN EMPOWER

I've always liked being able to offer others leadership opportunities they've never had before, especially since my network is full of pioneering people of color. When you're in PR, you can often do that. You can select a spokesperson within an organization who may be great at their craft but has never been recognized as a leader. I've learned that most journalists don't want to talk to the CEO about something specific. They want to speak to the person "on the ground"—the program manager, widget-maker, or data analyst who can share insights from the numbers. PR pros have the ability to train all kinds of people for storytelling opportunities or give them the recognition they may have never received before.

If you manage volunteer programs, you can appoint people to be leaders in committees where they can learn new skills or share strengths they may not be able to in their current roles. True PR pros become trusted advisers to top leadership at organizations, meaning we can be champions of social responsibility as well as diversity, equity, and inclusion (DEI) initiatives. You can use your "stage" to offer individuals from disenfranchised backgrounds opportunities to be seen and heard. That's just a glimpse of how we can create social good as PR pros. What positive systemic changes can you make from the systems you actually build? If it's your PR strategy or program, you have the power to create real positive change!

When I worked in diversity and inclusion at H-E-B, one of the major events I managed was the company's participation in the Martin Luther King Jr. march. The MLK March in San Antonio is said to be the largest in the country. Before I was hired, there were about 125 employees participating. I analyzed the program the company had in place and realized the logistics could be improved to encourage more participation. They hadn't offered transportation for employees to get to the march, and the route looked difficult to navigate. Using a people-first mindset, I looked for ways to make it easier for employees and their family members (many off from school) to participate.

PRO TIP

Whenever you can *bring* your audience to your event, they're more likely to show up!

My department made budgetary and logistic adjustments to remove barriers to employee participation. We asked everyone to meet at a nearby H-E-B store, provided a store-catered breakfast (benefitting store sales and removing a lack of breakfast as an obstacle), and escorted employees and any of their participating family or friends to the march on buses. That year we had over 400 employees represent the company in the march, becoming a sea of company red that shined bright on the front page of the next day's newspaper. The key to identifying the barriers to participation and removing them was developing a new MLK March volunteer committee. Because we created that citywide committee, I was able to listen to, work with, and empower individuals across departments, stores, and facilities to put on the march. Those employees who generously volunteered their time became the staff I didn't have, and for some of them, that committee work put a little more purpose into their days. As a PR pro, you're always able to help others, even when they're helping you.

WRITING AND EDITING ARE FUNDAMENTAL

Being a strong writer is very important in this work. We're always creating copy for press kits, websites, scripts, speeches, brochures, and more. In PR, you can't just be a "good writer" or even a creative writer like I was. You have to be proficient at writing in **Associated Press (AP) style** to be a good PR writer. Journalists use AP style in their writing, so anything a PR person writes for a journalist, like media materials, should follow the same rules on grammar, punctuation, numbers, and so on. That was a surprise to me when I started as a PR coordinator. I knew MLA style from college, but that wasn't the style my boss was asking me to write in.

I quickly learned that most of what I knew about writing from college was useless. I was going to be judged harshly by journalists if I couldn't create press materials that followed AP style rules. Time to reach out for help. One of my then-co-workers, Lorraine Pulido, PhD, was teaching an evening "writing for PR" class at a local university and allowed me to sit in. I went to her class twice a week after work, did all the assignments, and learned all the essential writing rules and materials —well after my own college graduation.

If you don't know AP style, take your own class or online course right away. There are even cheat sheets online. Writing and editing in AP style makes journalists' lives easier, which is the foundation of good media relations. Get an AP Stylebook online membership and use it. Also, continue to take writing classes and test your skills throughout your career. Nothing kills PR cred like bad grammar or spelling.

PR IS FOR EVERYONE

Any subject, business sector, or even hobby you're interested in can have a PR job related to it. It's a field in which you can be a chameleon. PR provides a chance to tailor your communication style, content development, or even attire depending on who you're working with and why. There are a multitude of disciplines and services to use as you're doing work in this field. Specialties run the gamut, so take whatever you're passionate about and intersect it with PR. You'd better believe there's a PR pro for that! For instance, my former PR apprentice Alexandra Berg was a dancer. After she worked for my firm to develop a strong PR portfolio, she was able to find a full-time PR job—for the Charlotte Ballet! How cool is that?

As fun and similar as PR can be to other communication areas, PR is also different because it should be practiced following a code of ethics. (PRSA has a code of ethics on its website you can refer to for guidelines.) Practitioners should keep integrity, honesty, fairness, and serving the public at the forefront of all we do.

If you have a heart for people, want to champion a special cause, or just want to keep from getting bored in your career, you're in the right place! Each day is different, and unique perspectives help organizations better serve different types of stakeholders. Being able to establish, keep, and build relationships through win-win connections is special and should be seen that way.

GETTING STARTED IN PR

You get the degree; you get the dream job—right? Or you've worked in journalism, so transitioning into PR should be easy—right? Any working PR practitioner can tell you the on-ramp isn't that clear. Employers say a relevant bachelor's degree and/or journalism experience is necessary to apply, but that's just part of what they're looking for. Learning the *theory* of PR and being in the *practice* of it can be very different. Experience counts for a lot. In a time of social unrest, recurring disruptions, and shrinking newsrooms, the demand is high for strategic PR professionals. Employers are looking for PR strategists who can guide them through turbulent times, and that often necessitates real-world experience. Someone applying for a PR role without hands-on experience or a portfolio could remain jobless for a long time.

There are seven principles that can help aspiring pros prepare to earn (and keep) a place in the PR world.

1. Be Flexible to Move Forward

Everyone has to start somewhere. Sometimes new grads have to take a job—any job—so they can move closer to what they want to be doing. Or an established reporter or marketing professional may need to make a lateral job move or even take a pay cut to get into their first PR role. My first job after college graduation was as a grant writer at a tiny, now-closed nonprofit museum. It allowed me to learn some communication skills and pay my loans while I kept looking for my first PR opportunity. I free-lanced for a PR agency on top of my museum job to gain some PR experience. Soon, I was offered a full-time role at the agency, and I've been in PR ever since. Consider the skills that you could learn, work experience that could transfer, and connections you could make if you have to take a job outside of PR.

2. Build Your Personal Brand

Everything you do or don't do communicates something. What you post online, how you dress, how you speak, how you write, how you manage your nonverbals, and even how you eat matters. One of my job interviews was conducted over lunch so that they could see how I would represent the organization at meals! (I ordered a small cup of soup and barely touched it. Luckily, I had read that you're not really there to eat at meal interviews.) These are some of the ways others perceive your brand or you as a professional. Build your personal brand intentionally early on, and be prepared to manage it your entire career.

3. Develop Two-Way Relationships

Network with other professionals with the purpose of building relationships. You'll reap endless rewards by simply being helpful to others. Be a team player at work, a resource for industry colleagues, and a source for journalists. They'll remember you…in a good way! It's not really *who* you know; it's *how* they know you that counts.

4. Keep Up with Technology and Trends

Technology has changed how we do PR work and how we measure its impact. If you don't keep up with technology and PR trends, you can't be an effective professional. School will never be out in this career. Go curate the education you really need to be successful.

5. Do More than Is Required

Problem-solve, overdeliver, and always do your best whenever you have a chance to work in a PR capacity. That's doubly true if you're trying to get your first shot in the field. Make sure your best is *actually* good by asking for feedback. If you're interning, get out of your cube and ask how you can help. Young professionals have an unfair stereotype of lacking soft skills such as conversing with others. Stand out to get a reference or a lead at the next job up for grabs. If you're working as a reporter or in another field, join the local PRSA chapter in your area to start **networking** and making contacts with PR pros. Or, join the board or a committee to get hands-on PR practice. Attend their events or other PR industry events to get professional PR education, make new PR pals and learn about upcoming job openings.

6. Get Creative to Get Experience

How can you get PR experience if you have already graduated or are already working full time? Volunteer at a nonprofit or with a PR committee to start practicing PR in a low-risk situation. Or, try freelancing as a side hustle to your current job to start building a PR portfolio (as long as there's not a conflict of interest). Organizations, agencies, and independent PR pros are always looking for outside contract help. If you're no longer a college student but are open to learning, ask about being an apprentice. My firm has helped several college graduates gain experience under this model. Be creative in how you get experience, and then be creative in solving problems as a PR pro.

7. Make the Most of Every Opportunity

When you have a shot, take it! Put all of your energy into learning everything you can and impressing anyone you can. Show appreciation for others' knowledge, time, and referrals. People will want to help you if they know you welcome their assistance.

Shoring up your PR knowledge and experience gaps as early in your career as possible will help you feel more competent in a field where excellence is required. PR is much more complex, multidisciplined, and stressful than most people know. How we perform work and what we're responsible for constantly change. There are some fundamentals, though, so the following chapters will explain the most essential areas of PR.

CHAPTER 1 TAKEAWAYS

To recap the essentials of this chapter, remember these main points and terms:

1. PR work involves more than just media relations.
2. Your background and interests can be leveraged as assets in this field.
3. Shoring up your deficits by gaining experience or getting specific education will help you feel more competent in a field where trust is paramount.

Important Terms:

- **Associated Press (AP) style:** The writing style guide used in journalism, which dictates rules for grammar, punctuation, numbers, and more.

- **Marketing:** The activity, set of institutions, and processes for creating, communicating, delivering, and exchanging offerings (goods and services) that have value for customers, clients, partners and society at large.
- **Media relations:** Working with journalists to build positive relationships and earn publicity.
- **PRSA:** The Public Relations Society of America, a trade association.
- **Public relations:** A strategic communication process that builds mutually beneficial relationships between organizations and their publics.
- **Publicity:** Earning unpaid positive media coverage in outlets like newspapers, radio, TV, magazines, online publications, or podcasts.
- **Stakeholders:** People who matter to your organization.

PASS THE MIC 🎤:
AMELIA FOLKES, APR

Amelia Folkes is an award-winning PR professional and strategic communicator with a vision for helping brands solve communication challenges and achieve measurable results within changing, complex environments. She has more than 15 years of experience guiding clients in the technology, government, B2B/B2C, financial services, and nonprofit sectors. This experience includes work in crisis communications, stakeholder relations, thought leadership, and brand reputation management.

Q. What barriers may inhibit more diverse students or pros from working in PR?

A. Many colleges don't have a stand-alone PR offering, but instead, they offer classes within another degree program. This is why we need to introduce the career option earlier. For example, many students have never heard of PR, and by the time they are in college, it could be too late. Aspiring PR pros whose colleges didn't have an actual PR degree program can get creative to learn from practicing professionals. For example, they can reach out to local PR or marketing agencies and ask for informational interviews so they can meet and find working

professionals and get involved with local professional associations with student chapters, whether it's PRSSA (student
chapter of PRSA), IABC (a communications organization),
or an advertising or marketing association. Or, students can
reach out to a local professional society or trade association
focused on PR, communications, or marketing to inquire about
mentorship programs, internships, or shadow opportunities.
What helped me was having a professional to talk to, so I could
ask them what the career was like and for advice on how to
succeed. When they do start working in PR, they should reach
out to students in English, journalism, communication, and
marketing departments to help introduce them to the field.

CHAPTER 2

~~/

Start Smart with PR Etiquette

First impressions count in any industry, but in PR, they are especially important. If you care about building relationships with people, you need to care about how they actually *relate* to you. Creating relationships with people begins with the first impression we make. Where did someone meet you? What mood were you in? Did you act bored at that networking event? Did you call the newsroom in a panic wondering why a news crew wasn't at your press conference? Any kind of impression we make, particularly when it's our initial one, can have lasting effects.

When I first started in PR, I was freelancing nights and weekends in addition to my new, full-time grant-writing job. I really wanted to work in PR, but I didn't have success finding a position and needed a full-time job upon graduation to start paying off my college loans. I accepted a grant writer position knowing that it would offer communication experience and that I would learn skills I could add to my resume. One chance conversation with a spin instructor at my gym helped me find a way to start working in the field. I told him I really wanted to work in PR, but I hadn't learned much about it in college, nor did I know anyone who worked in the field. There weren't any positions in the newspaper (they were an important source of job openings back then), so I wasn't sure what to do. He actually *did* know someone, so he connected me with a PR agency owner who needed some freelance help. She gave me the opportunity to freelance for her to gain experience in PR. This would be work I did in addition to my full-time job. With a little direction, I set off to figure out how to do PR on my own.

I fit in some (bad) writing, media pitching through email, and media phone call follow-ups outside of my regular work schedule. The very first time I called the TV assignment's desk at our Fox station affiliate, the call was answered by one of the grumpiest voices in the business. I soon learned that if I caught News Director "Bob" on the line, he'd answer my questions, but it wouldn't be pretty. Bob answered the phone after a few rings, and I asked if he had seen an email about an upcoming special event. He didn't remember it, so he looked it up while I was on the phone. The very next thing he said was, "Don't you know you're not supposed to put *all* the new stations in the 'To' line of your email?"

I felt as stupid as he made me sound because *of course I didn't* know that. I thought I was being efficient by sending the media alert to all the media at once. Why should I email each and every news desk separately when I could grab all the email addresses, put them in the "To" line, and get the job done? There are many ways to make PR work more efficient that come off as rude or lazy to journalists. There are cultural norms and nuances that aren't taught in the classroom or even in most PR books. I certainly haven't read about being careful how I email journalists in a textbook—even when I recently studied for my Accreditation in Public Relations (APR)!

No one told me there was a certain way I should email journalists so that every pitch feels tailored only for them. PR pros never want to seem like they're cold calling everyone or trying too hard either. Pitching a story idea is a bit like dating. A pitch, short for "sales pitch," is best aimed at a specific target when you have a good shot. Like I learned as a rookie, sending a mass email to several reporters at once looks spammy. Ideally, each pitch should be customized and sent to each news outlet or reporter individually. That takes research, thoughtfulness, and time. An individualized pitch to the Fox station would have made a better impression on Bob. From then on, I felt like a nitwit every time I called his desk, but I still called. He probably forgot all about me, but I never forgot the lesson he taught me. I took email management very seriously from then on. I've even taken a class on it!

BUILDING TRUST

To be seen as a true guide or adviser in PR, you have to work very hard at building trust. That starts the first moment you meet a new journalist, potential client, or colleague in the business. Some things I've learned that help build trust are to stay away from gossip, to keep confidential things confidential, and not to exaggerate, overestimate, or guesstimate when you don't have the answer. Go find the answer!

To build trust, make sure everything you write, create, and share is factual. Verify stats. Verify the spelling of names and programs. Verify any proper noun that you use. Verify what's proprietary information, and always manage a flow of communication between your organization and others. I suggest you verify, *then* trust. Manage the expectations superiors and journalists have of you by overdelivering whenever you can. If your word is seen as solid and you tactfully tell people the hard truth, that also builds trust. In our business, trust makes you a resource, earns you a seat at the decision-making table, and will help you rise to earn the big bucks as you guide others through the trickiest of situations, issues, and crises.

FOLLOW THE NEWS

When a PR pro says they don't watch or read the news, it's as hypocritical as a dietitian who doesn't eat vegetables. Not following the news is a huge mistake some PR pros make. Just the other day, I was following up with an education reporter and was able to congratulate her on the front-page story she had written. She was flattered that I had noticed it, and I was able to connect my story pitch with a topic she was clearly interested in. She thought I was absolutely on point with my story idea and went on to pitch it as a feature story opportunity to her editor. Following the news enabled me to show this journalist I was familiar with her, the type of stories she wrote, and what was trending in her beat. Now I'm potentially a resource to her, not a PR salesperson. In PR, if you're not at least scanning the newspaper, watching some TV news, or listening to talk radio, it's almost impossible to be strategic with media relations work. Knowing what journalists may like starts with understanding their world and the audience they serve. Working with journalists, pitching and securing news stories, and handling their needs is what media relations is built on. If you follow the news, you'll be able to discover story ideas, news segments that offer story opportunities, or information on the journalists you can leverage in your pitching. Start following the news in the market areas you do or will work in at the minimum.

DO YOUR RESEARCH

My cell phone just rang with a spam call about suspicious activity on my bitcoin account. I don't *have* a bitcoin account! If the spammers had done their research, they would have figured out something more likely to get me to hand over my confidential information. When PR pros don't do their research, they can look just as foolish and make a terrible first impression.

No PR pro starts out as an expert on the category they're representing. You often have to do quick research in the beginning. If you work inside a company (or in-house) you can quickly deepen your knowledge on the category or organization. If you work for a PR agency, you may be juggling several client accounts at once. Becoming an expert on a certain category, like education or technology, can take longer.

During my agency days, I never knew who or what I'd be talking about at any given time. In a single day, I've represented a published poet, a nationwide nonprofit, Lactaid milk, and a local real estate developer. I've shared stories about comedians, kids who needed mentors, bankers, and Green Berets. I am *not* an expert in all these industry areas, and I let my clients know that right from the start. I'm a communication expert, and through research and communication planning, I identify who to bring forward as the topic expert.

First, I learn as much as I can about the topic or the person I'm working with. Then, I make sure the client has a well-spoken spokesperson who can explain the details. That spokesperson should be a **subject matter expert (SME)** journalists can interview or someone we can rely on to give us information needed for writing materials or producing content. An SME is a person at an organization who knows their featured service, program, or offering best. Depending on the informational need, that role could be a program manager, a scientist, a teacher, or a CEO. It depends on the story or scenario.

Do your own research to be able to communicate on any topic in a trustworthy way. Often, experiential learning will help you learn quickly. For me, that meant signing up as a Big Sister mentor myself, eating the restaurant's food, or sampling the lactose-free milk. Anytime I spoke from my personal experience, listeners were much more interested in what I had to say. Try out the thing you say is so great to be sure it really is. Your personal stories and experiences will be more enticing than anything shared from an outside perspective. Your experience can also help you share any user issues or operational improvements and can help you come up with PR ideas. As you do your research, learn how terms are spelled and capitalized, who is in charge where, what info may be confidential, and who to turn to for SME support.

PICK UP THE PHONE!

Some people hate talking on the phone. I hear this often from younger pros who grew up using their phones for everything but making calls. Sure, picking up the phone to call a reporter or handle a sensitive issue can be nerve-racking. It still has to be done. PR pros have to communicate well on the phone to do their jobs well.

There's so much more information you can exchange verbally on a call. You can figure out someone's tone, share friendly banter to build rapport before you jump into business, or brainstorm in a more collaborative way than you can when you're sending information through email or text. Plus, if you do media relations, you should be making and taking calls from journalists all the time.

We do text a lot as PR pros, but don't make the mistake of using text so much it becomes the only way you use your phone. Texting wasn't around when I started working in PR, but it's become very useful for work over the years. From my experience, the COVID-19 pandemic accelerated the use of texting between journalists and PR pros. In the past, you'd have to be on the BFF level to have a journalist's cell phone number. PR pros needed to call news desks or a reporter's office line. When the pandemic hit, journalists had to work remotely, so getting in touch by cell became the norm. I've coordinated entire stories with a journalist through text because they had loud kids at home or were in a loud environment where hearing each other would be too difficult. Texting can be useful, but it should only be one way you communicate on the phone.

I'm glad some of the walls have come down between the PR and journalism fields and that we're swapping mobile numbers more often. However, texting should still be seen as an intimate form of communication. Sending a text is like tapping someone on the shoulder. If you weren't on that level with a person before, or if what you're texting about isn't urgent, you should probably reconsider your method. It's still more workplace-appropriate to send an email or make a phone call to someone so they can respond with less interruption. I actually ask people for permission to text them first whenever that's possible. Figuring out people's communication preferences, especially on a tool as close by as a phone, shows you're a considerate professional.

PRO TIP

People often send calls to voicemail if they don't know the number that is dialing in. Leave a detailed voicemail stating who you are and what you want. Then, follow up with a text sharing that same info. That increases the likelihood of getting a response in some way.

EMAIL MANAGEMENT STRATEGY

One mistake people make with **digital communication**—communicating online via email, text, social media, messaging tools, or video platforms—is not taking it as seriously as other forms of communication. Using correct spelling and punctuation, watching our tone, and timing always matter. Email communication is used (and abused) most in the workplace, so being strategic about using email effectively is important. According to technology website LifeWire, the average office worker receives 120 emails each day. Journalists probably receive twice that many; many of them are pitches from PR practitioners. Here are specific email rules to help you send better emails:

PRO TIP

Use exclamations sparingly in emails (and only use one at a time). Not everything needs to be emphasized!! Don't you just hate this!!!

1. Watch Your Tone

So much of our work is communicated through email. We introduce ourselves, share a story idea, or send written documentation through most of the workday. Our work is often remote from others we work with, like journalists or social media influencers. You might never meet some of the people you send emails to in person. Tone is hard to interpret in emails, but people usually interpret it based on the content, capitalization, and punctuation. Why can't you understand my point? DOESN'T THIS FEEL MORE INTENSE THAN THE LAST SENTENCE? Do you understand why punctuation matters?!

Lose any sarcasm and vagueness in your emails. Be clear. Use positive words to frame a positive conversation, and use punctuation with the understanding that each type asks a question(?), makes a statement(.), or makes a declaration(!).

Using an emoji can help with tone, but use them sparingly (especially in more formal workplaces). Be sure they are easy to interpret and do not have alternative meanings. Something simple like ☺ may be fine.

2. Take Complex Topics Offline

If you need to ask several questions or need to discuss something complex, call somebody and have a conversation. Then, follow up with an email if you need to confirm your understanding or share additional links, attachments, or information in writing. Don't copy someone else on the email if the topic is confidential or sensitive.

PRO TIP

Follow the directions you receive in an email. If you're asked to reply all, then reply all. If you're asked to reply only to the sender, do that. Attention to detail is important in PR, and following directions in an email is a basic courtesy to extend.

---

3. Keep It Short and Sweet

With email, the shorter, friendlier and more direct, the better. Get in, get to business, and get out of that email you're writing. Make sure you have a signature line that includes your name, title, company, and phone number for journalists or other stakeholders you're working with who may need to get in touch with you quickly. Some people include their websites, social media handles, and more. Consider making a couple of different signature options to use—one with a phone number and one without. Think through your signature, and use it based on whom you're emailing with and why.

Remember not to email when you're feeling angry or frustrated. Don't get into email fights with others or trash talk someone in an email. It's so easy to accidentally reply all, or someone can forward on your comments. PR pros should not make those mistakes. Sensitive information and private conversations are best shared offline.

4. Edit Before Sending

There is always a way to check your message clarity, spelling, or grammar usage before you send out an email. Outlook has those tool settings, and apps like Grammarly can be installed in a Chrome browser to help check for mistakes in all kinds of email programs. You can even set up delays so you have a chance to double-check important emails before they are sent. Also, ask a trusted colleague to read over an email if you're struggling with the message copy. A second opinion can help you revise something you feel unsure about.

5. Think Before You Send

Emails can help or harm your career. It's important to recognize that unless you own the company, you don't own the email. Don't send or receive anything that would embarrass you later. That means don't send any explicit language, photos, rude comments, racist remarks, or tasteless jokes. EVER. Make sure your clients and colleagues understand this, too. I've seen some naughty and nasty things come out about industry pros based on their work email exchanges. Behave yourself in email (and everywhere else) if you care about your reputation. Reputation is everything if you want to do well in PR.

6. Follow the To, CC, and BCC Rules

Use the right email field appropriately to stay in line with email etiquette. Here's how to choose whose email address to put in which email field before you hit send:

- **To:** Use this field when you're speaking to the receiver directly and the content of the email is meant for them.
- **CC:** Short for "carbon copy." Use this field to include other people as observers to the email information or conversation. This helps people who were copied follow a conversation because it's relevant to them, but being copied indicates they are more of an observer of the conversation, not an active part of the direct communication exchange. Only CC people when they need to be involved in the message or if you have been asked to include them. Before your first email with a new client or team, ask your supervisor or point of contact who they prefer to include. If you're at an agency, you may need to ask who should be included in the email according to each topical message. If you receive an email where someone is copied, do reply all (unless you're asked not to) to keep them in the loop. For example, sometimes I ask people to keep one of my team members copied by leaving them in the CC, and the replier doesn't. They just reply back to me. That means

I need to forward emails now to keep my team member updated, which slows our communication exchange.

- **BCC:** A "blind carbon copy" field should be used to make someone aware of a message without their email address being seen. This field is good to use when you have to send one email from your inbox to multiple people who don't know each other. Some people use it to make someone aware of a conversation without exposing the fact that they were informed. When you do that, you risk the BCC person replying all and blowing your cover. If you personally get an email as a BCC, be careful how you reply. Never hit reply all. I prefer to forward emails or start a new email conversation if I'm ever unsure of what may happen with a BCC.

The previous six tips cover the most egregious email-use violations. Manage your email manners to make yourself look professional, effective, and pleasant.

COMMAND YOUR CALENDAR

Managing your calendar will seem impossible some days, but try to be on top of it as often as possible. People who show up to meetings a little bit early seem like competent professionals just by their punctuality. Know how to use calendar software to make appointments, invite others to appointments, and remind yourself where you need to be throughout the day.

When I was in high school, my marching band director would always say, "To be on time is to be early." He was right. You have to arrive a few minutes early to be set up to start on time. I personally struggle with punctuality when it comes to in-person events. I try to squeeze in too many things in my day, so I'm often five to ten minutes late to in-person meetups. Every time I arrive late for a lunch or coffee meeting, I pay the tab as my penance. That's helped me remember to take time seriously, and it shows the other person I do value their company.

Since Zoom became a new meeting place option, being on time has become a lot easier! Unless you're in a meeting that's running late, there's really no reason to be late for virtual meetings. If you need to, set your meetings with alerts that remind you to prep and arrive with time to spare.

As PR people, it may be our job to pull high-level executives out of situations where it's hard for them to remove themselves in order to get them to their next meetings, but managing ourselves shouldn't be as difficult. Invest in an assistant to help with managing your schedule, if needed. Even Siri, my iPhone virtual assistant, helps me stay on top of things. Find a system that works for you so you can maintain positive relationships with peers, reporters, clients, and bosses. Whatever calendar you use, sync it up with your phone, and keep it updated. I've found a paper calendar alone is not enough to keep up with all the moving parts of a PR day.

NEVER GHOST IN BUSINESS

Ghosting, or not responding to emails, phone calls, or texts, is the new passive-aggressive way too many people use to opt out of saying they're uncomfortable with something. I used to see it more in my personal life. Now, it's happening more often in the business world. Professionals, even professional communicators, are choosing silence as a response. Don't do it!

Because relationships are paramount to our business, ghosting is irresponsible. If you want a relationship with someone, have the courtesy to craft and send a response, even if it's uncomfortable.

As a PR pro, if you have to decline someone's offer, whether personal or professional, just say the hard thing. Say it kindly; say it promptly—just say it. The tension created by making that person wait for a response or follow-up is more damaging to your relationship than being straightforward. It's perfectly acceptable to tell another person that plans have changed, that an expense is outside of your budget, or that you're not able to assist them right now. Being clear will help you maintain a positive reputation and give them the resolution they need to move on.

Even if journalists don't respond to your emails, do not ghost *them* if they email you. As you get to know each journalist, you'll learn their response style. For most, no response means they can't cover it. But sometimes, they haven't seen the email yet. That's why picking up the phone and giving them a call to gauge their interest is helpful if a pitch is important. Sometimes they did miss the email or didn't like your angle. You can often brainstorm another option together on the phone.

PRO TIP

You *will* get ghosted by journalists at some point when you're pitching them story ideas. You'll hear time and again that they don't have time to respond to the hundreds of emails they get daily. Offer grace because that's a nuance of how they must work to manage their time.

DON'T BURN BRIDGES

Our job as PR professionals is to be connectors. We build bridges between groups to share information, needs, and resources. That's my favorite part of this profession. However, you can't be a good connector if you're pissing people off. Try your hardest not to burn down any bridge you're on. That means you shouldn't walk out on a job unless you absolutely never want to go there again and every one of the individuals you worked with no longer matters to you on any level. Your professional reputation will be built based on your behaviors, and one bad moment can follow you everywhere like a bad stink.

Stay on your best behavior whenever you can because in PR you never know who you are going to work with. For example, you won't see me getting into social media arguments or posting political content. I try to stay kind, positive, collaborative, and encouraging. No one can really complain about my online behavior. I've run back into, worked with, or even worked for people I knew from childhood, college, and past jobs. It would be a shame if someone you flamed was someone you needed in the future.

PRO TIP

Asking "What's your deadline?" can help in lots of different situations. Sometimes we put too much pressure on ourselves to drop everything and do something right away. That's not always necessary. Prioritizing is important in PR.

BE RESPONSIVE

Not everyone likes me, and not everyone in your workplace will like you. Earning respect is a better goal to strive for. I'm known for working hard and getting the job done despite any challenges. At my firm, MVW Communications, we like to move quickly. While sometimes we may have projects that fall into a "hurry up and wait" mode, our team is never the cause of bottlenecks or lag time. Being responsive helps keep projects and people moving along. Try to get back to people via email in one to two business days, and respond to texts or online messages within a couple hours, if possible. Even just acknowledging you received the message and will get back to the other person by a certain date or time is helpful.

Even in a meeting, a verbal acknowledgment is appreciated. Saying something like "Got it—I'll work on that. By when do you need it?" will help you seem responsive. Show you care, and it'll go a long way.

CHAPTER 2 TAKEAWAYS

To recap the essentials of this chapter, remember these main points and terms:

1. Start building a positive personal brand by being attentive to details and responsive.
2. Watch how you email with others by following email etiquette.
3. Manage your communication style to build bridges, even if others around you don't.

Important Terms:

- **BCC:** Use the "blind carbon copy" field in email when you want to protect the privacy of recipients' email addresses.
- **CC:** Use the "carbon copy" field in email when someone should be included in the email exchange as an observer to the conversation.
- **Digital communication:** Communicating online via email, text, social media, messaging tools, or video platforms.
- **Ghosting:** Not responding to emails, phone calls, texts, or other forms of communication.
- **Subject matter expert (SME):** A person at an organization who knows a featured service, program, or offering best and can be trained for media interviews.

PASS THE MIC 🎤:
ANAIS BIERA MIRACLE

Anais Biera Miracle is the Chief Communications Officer for one of the largest Latino-led nonprofit organizations in the US. Anais oversees the Communications and National Strategic Partnerships departments and has more than 17 years' experience in public relations. Anais's expertise is in strategic communications, media relations, crisis communications, public affairs, and branding.

Q. What role does mentoring play in our success as PR pros?

A. As PR pros, mentorship has to be the core of our profession. Early in our careers, we may need to be sponsored to get our first job or reach that next level. Mentors can also cultivate a level of competence in us. We have to be willing to ask for help and learn from others who have more experience or new strategies to share. It's also our responsibility to set an example for others and offer support however we can. It may be difficult to constantly learn, but that's what good PR professionals do to adapt to the ever-changing PR landscape.

CHAPTER 3

~~~~

Media Relations Do's and Don'ts

THE FIRST DISCIPLINE MOST PEOPLE THINK OF WHEN THEY hear "PR" is media relations. It may not be all we do, but it's probably the hardest thing we do. It's also the sexiest to talk about because it's full of uncertainty, thrilling wins, and public losses. The only way to consistently *win* in media relations is when you embrace two strategies: being proactive and understanding it will never be easy.

I've worked with journalists since my first days in PR. While I have many industry awards that show I'm good at it, it's still very challenging work. So much of ensuring a successful outcome is out of my control. Unless you pay for coverage—which is really advertising—you can't ever control if, when, or how a story is reported on. Even journalists can't control some aspects of the work, since they have editors who dictate what goes out and when. Because of the uncertain nature of it all, media relations is not something any pro finds *easy* to do.

If you're working in PR, you will probably work with the media. Just accept that it's work full of uncomfortable moments. Working with journalists (or trying to) can be intimidating even when you're good at it. Everything we send, say, or share with a journalist can help or hurt us (and our organizations). In media relations, a PR person is often a salesperson, a connector, a fact finder, and at times, a gatekeeper. If you work to build proactive relationships with journalists, you could also be seen as an ally or a source. Even still, journalists often relocate for jobs or leave the field, so even the strongest relationships you make can be short-lived.

The smartest strategy to take when working with journalists is to *always be proactive—not reactive*—in media relations. You should be intentionally building relationships and sharing relevant story opportunities, not waiting for journalists to call. Media relations should be a game of mostly offense, with a little defense needed at times. To play offense, you need to get out there and make relationships with journalists in person and online. As you get to know journalists, you can proactively reach out to them with relevant story ideas, organizational updates, and different ways to work together. Too many organizations don't keep an ongoing dialogue with journalists. Some organizations even have leadership who dislike working with journalists. When journalists don't know an organization and its people well, there's more room for error in reporting. That's where reactive and negative experiences begin.

Once, a business owner came to me for help after receiving some negative media coverage. The owner was building a new restaurant in a historic neighborhood, which caused tension in the community. The owner had not been proactive in working with the media. Journalists who were covering the restaurant and economic development beats were requesting information but not getting a response. As a result, those journalists put together stories based on information they found through public records and observation. Missing from those stories was the restaurant's valuable perspective and important details. If the client had proactively invited journalists to interview them or had released press materials laying out the facts, the coverage could have begun in a more positive way. Then this client would not have needed to spend as much time and money hiring consultants to clean up the reputation damage.

This chapter will walk you through how to be proactive and planful when tackling media relations. This methodology will help you become more confident when trying to earn media coverage or when answering their inquiries.

MEDIA COVERAGE
SHAPES BRAND PERCEPTION

Despite the talk of media mistrust, journalists still serve as influential figures in our society. According to the Pew Research Center, Americans tend to judge whether a story is trustworthy or not based primarily on the news outlet that distributed it. However, individual journalists can become authorities in their own right. Many journalists freelance for multiple outlets, so their influence can be felt across multiple mediums. When an outlet puts out a story, third-party credibility is transferred onto that story. If it's a positive story, that can enhance an organization's image. If it's negative, it can damage it. No content an organization creates itself will have that same sentimental value or social proof.

Certainly, we work with journalists to serve up news updates and garner positive reactions. Hopefully, that's most of the work pros do—enhance a brand's image or a leader's image. By humanizing the organization through stories, we can build emotional equity and begin to inspire brand champions to support the brand. There can be a lot of love between an organization and its stakeholders when there is good publicity about it. When (not if) something bad does happen, that positive image is like a cushion for the organization that helps buffer negative blowback.

PR professionals at any level want to build awareness of their organization and keep them top of mind with their customers. But it's just as important to keep those organizations top of mind for journalists. If a journalist doesn't think of you or your organization as a **source**—a responsive, trustworthy resource to get information or story ideas from—you're probably still managing a reactive media relations program. This means you're chasing coverage rather than managing a give-ask relationship with journalists (there's no *take* because demanding a story is unethical). You'll know you are becoming a source when reporters come to you for story ideas or to request interviews. Then you're leading the way!

GETTING STARTED WITH OUTREACH

Media relations is the work we do to build relationships with journalists and their media outlets. A good PR person should be in a proactive mode when working with journalists (a.k.a. reporters or the media). To get started with outreach, remember that planning is crucial.

Plan for Effective Media Relations

Effective media relations outreach begins with planning and ends with delivering a clear, impactful message that benefits your organization. My framework for effective media relations includes these 15 steps:

1. Define media coverage goals.
2. Research story angles.
3. Research which journalists may like the topic/beat.
4. Research which journalists have covered the organization before.
5. Create a targeted media list.
6. Write the pitch(es).
7. Write talking points and create necessary press kit materials.
8. Determine pitch strategies.
9. Pitch via email or phone and/or in person.
10. Train the spokesperson(s).
11. Coordinate interviews (when/where/how/who).
12. Support the spokesperson during the interviews (on-site coaching, taking pics for social media use).
13. Ensure the journalist receives all the information, interviews, and visuals they need for their story.
14. Monitor story coverage (to evaluate for sentiment and save for your media recap).
15. Evaluate the effectiveness of the spokesperson(s) and share what could be done better in the next interview.

Using this strategic framework can help you plan a robust media outreach campaign. Or the steps can serve as a checklist for a more tactical pitching opportunity. Strategic media relations steps should be followed to serve both your organization and the journalists' needs. Taking care of both parties helps support a positive experience for all. When the experience is positive, the story often comes out as a win for the organization, and your relationship with the reporter is strengthened. The better you get at managing media relations, the more likely it is that journalists will want to work with you.

We'll go into more detail on some of these fundamental steps in this chapter and review the writing of press kit materials in Chapter 8.

Media Coverage Goals

Before you begin any media relations campaign, you should determine your media coverage goals. What are you trying to achieve? What's the motivation for putting yourself or your organization in the position to work with the media? It's not always comfortable!

The first reason an organization may want to work with the media is to try to satisfy its messaging needs in a proactive manner. For example, when a company is building a new headquarters, they may want to share updates and certain milestones with a large audience at specific times. Or a company may need to get in front of an emerging crisis like an oceanic oil spill by providing factual information to help mitigate misinformation.

Another important goal for media coverage is to share positive news and build brand equity with journalists and the community. Similar to managing our physical health, proactive management of an organization's reputation is much easier to maintain than trying to rebuild what's lost. Sometimes, reputation damage can't be repaired until the journalist moves on or a lot of time, effort, and money are spent.

Pitching Story Ideas

When you share a story idea with a reporter, that's called sending them a **pitch.** Most pitches are sent via email, but pitching can happen in person, over the phone, or in social media messages. I've even successfully pitched an idea to a reporter in the bathroom! Pitching is when you share a concise message about a story opportunity and why it should be covered. It's your attempt to sell an idea and see if the journalist is interested. And it's certainly a pitch—throwing out an idea to see if journalists are interested in taking a swing at it.

This "sales process" is one of the hardest aspects of media relations for PR pros. From pitching, following up, and coordinating a story, it feels like you're working to quickly close a deal before some imaginary window closes.

After you pitch a story, allow for a waiting period to see if the reporter bites. I try to give them a response window of a business week before I check back in. Most times, you'll have to **follow**

up with the journalist to see what they think. Or find out if they even saw the email! Following up isn't comfortable, especially on the phone. It's easy to feel like a solicitor when you know you're calling someone unannounced.

Even after all these years, I still have to psych myself up before I dial. It's uncomfortable, but every single time I've made the effort to call a journalist, it's helped me highlight the story opportunity, build rapport, or find out what breaking news is stealing the show. Then I'm able to tell the client what news they're competing with for coverage or what breaking news story is in the way. There's an old saying about news coverage: "If it bleeds, it leads." Simply put, traumatic or dramatic news tends to get coverage at the top of the news hour. Many times, that's a fire, shooting, or bad car accident. When such news happens unexpectedly, it's called **breaking news,** and breaking news can derail your interview or press conference plans. This is why you'll always have to be flexible and solution-oriented whenever you do media relations.

Know What's Newsworthy

Understanding what is **newsworthy** is the mark of a stellar PR pro. Learning what's deemed worthy of news coverage comes with time and some embarrassing moments. Most pros figure out what's newsworthy after they get multiple story ideas shot down or have the excruciating experience of holding a press conference where no reporters show up.

Luckily for me, I was able to quickly pick up on the patterns of what seemed newsworthy to journalists. When you know what's newsworthy, you're able to filter out the bad story ideas from the good. (Believe me, some of your clients or bosses will think *everything* is newsworthy.) Once you understand the newsworthy criteria, you can conceptualize **story angles**—or multiple ways to approach one story topic—that will be in alignment with the criteria journalists look for.

Explaining what was newsworthy was always hard for me to articulate to others who wanted media relations advice. Then one day I found a list of the criteria that succinctly explained newsworthiness. *The Media & Culture: Mass Communication in a Digital Age* textbook lists eight criteria for newsworthiness based on journalism culture. To modernize this, I added a point of my own that has emerged in recent social-media-saturated years.

Below are nine ways that journalists determine which stories are worth covering. Use these points as criteria for whether you should consider your "news" worthy of a story pitch. A newsworthy story angle includes at least one of the following criteria. The more points of criteria your pitch has, the stronger it will be!

PRO TIP

What people find intriguing about these points also works to make intriguing content. Consider referencing these points when you're creating social media or other forms of content.

1. **Timeliness:** Stories that just happened or occur in a period of time or season that is about to happen. Don't miss a timeliness window by overanalyzing your pitch or taking too long to line up a spokesperson or data. Examples include holiday stories, anniversary stories, or stories on a weather incident that just occurred.

2. **Proximity:** Stories about local or nearby events/issues. If something big (like point #6) is happening regionally, nationally, or internationally, finding a local connection is a big win. Some outlets are hyper-local and only cover local news. Don't pitch a reporter in another city about something happening in your city that only impacts your city.

3. **Conflict:** Stories that seek/share opposing views. Examples include stories about opposing sides of a lawsuit, union strikes, or political conflict.

4. **Prominence:** Stories featuring prominent or influential people, such as the president visiting your nonprofit or the local philanthropist donating a life-changing amount of money.

5. **Human interest:** Extraordinary events that happen to ordinary people or ordinary people who are extraordinary because of their abilities or behaviors. An example would be the teacher who gave all his students bowties to raise their self-esteem or the child who raised thousands of dollars for the food bank at her birthday party.

6. **Consequence:** Stories about issues or events affecting many families and communities, such as the COVID-19 pandemic health crisis or a freeway shutdown.

7. **Usefulness:** Stories that have practicality and help people. Examples include job fairs or free food/clothing giveaways.

8. **Novelty and deviance:** Stories that happen outside the daily routine of life, such as someone who wins the Mega Millions lottery, a chicken becoming besties with a cat, or mass tragedy stories.

9. **Trends:** What's trending on social media has become a part of TV broadcast news, online articles, and even print articles. Something may be trending for any of the points above (especially #8). Journalists often

publish the posts or tweets if they have been posted publicly. For example, a cute kid's sassy video goes viral or Adidas shocks Twitter followers by posting a picture of 25 pairs of bare breasts. (That really happened.)

Understanding these points will help you know when you should pitch journalists or when you should not. If you're in planning mode, you can look for some of these newsworthy criteria points to include in your campaign. Or, you can even create an experience that hits on these points to make a story angle possible! You'll be a stronger "pitcher" and more respected in the newsrooms if you pitch based on these criteria.

Media List Creation

You can't send a pitch to journalists if you don't have their contact information. Then, if you don't target the right types of contacts, your outreach won't result in stories. The splatter approach of emailing your press release to everyone to see what sticks is not an effective strategy to take when pitching.

Putting together a media list isn't hard, but it can be time-consuming. You can start a simple one by creating a spreadsheet and inputting information about each major TV, radio, magazine, newspaper, and online outlet in the market area the organization you represent serves. How you make the list isn't as important as *who* you put it in. (I'll share tools for your *how* in Chapter 8.)

For most organizations, having a media list created based on the city they are headquartered in or the market area they serve is a good way to decide which journalists and outlets to include in a media list. This is considered a **location-based** list.

You may also want to make a **beat-based** list. Many journalists work within beats. A **beat** is like the subject area a journalist focuses on. For instance, a reporter may cover only technology stories. If you have a technology client or you work for a tech organization, you'll probably also want to find contact information for journalists who cover that beat. Targeting your pitches to journalists and news stations that either cover news that happens in your market area or news that is within their beat is how you'll want to approach media list research and creation.

PRO TIP

Prepare your organization for how to handle requests for interviews or information from the media. Establish a protocol for how to handle incoming calls or emails (route inquiries to the PR consultant or department).

Pitch Locally First

So many clients want national coverage. Whether it's ego or the thought that a large audience equals larger sales, that request is common. Work to manage the expectations around media relations by educating your clients on how media relations actually works.

It's likely you don't have a national story angle on your hands unless what you are doing impacts the entire nation. Always start by pitching local journalists. Where is your organization headquartered? That's typically seen as your local market. Journalists outside of your market area are not likely to care about what you're doing unless it directly impacts their audience.

Most cities want to know about their local heroes—the powerful companies and influential leaders who make the city better. It's great to be ambitious, but always try to point your effort in a productive direction. You'll get more media coverage if you're strategic and start with a local media approach.

Meet Journalists' Needs

Being willing to talk to journalists about their needs and story ideas can make all the difference in your media relations outreach. Just a little back-and-forth on the phone can help work out scheduling needs, help you brainstorm story ideas together, and let you get to know the reporter or station preferences better.

Ask about their communication preferences (email, calls, or texts), what types of stories they like to cover (if you can't figure that out yourself), and what their general work schedule is. That helps you send them information on stories they are more likely to be interested in through the tools and time frames they prefer. Tailoring your approach for each journalist and media outlet is a smart strategy for your media relations efforts. That's high-touch customer service that will help you develop a positive reputation with the media.

Be ready to take requests and make interviews happen even on the same day that you pitch. My phone has rung just minutes after an email was sent! Never pitch before you go into a big meeting or at a time you can't get to your phone or email. Not being able to respond and "close" the opportunity quickly could mean you lose the sale.

Part of our work as PR pros is understanding how journalists think, how they work, and what they need from us to do their jobs. If you can put yourself in their hypothetical shoes, you can be a strong media relations specialist. People can be lazy. Outwork your competitors by being a little nicer, more organized, and more of an ally to journalists. That will make you stand out in a good way.

Prepare the Spokesperson

For most interviews, the spokesperson should be the SME on the interview topic. They're the person who knows the most about the zoo habitats or restaurant operations or can share how their customers are dealing with shipping disruptions. The SME is the "driver of the story bus," as I tell clients, and they should be able to take any journalist on a mapped-out ride. Train yourself or your SMEs to be able to guide any journalist—from a rookie general assignment reporter to a veteran reporter who's covered the beat for decades—through a clear message. Spokespeople should not only answer questions; they should be able to deliver a compelling message and tell a story rich with colorful details and credible examples of what they're describing.

To help your SME do that, you must prepare their specific message in advance of any interview. If you follow my framework, the pitch you send to reporters should be full of content that is a part of the ultimate message you want a spokesperson to share. From that pitch, write a more expansive message on what you'd like the media to know. Then, edit that message down into talking points. **Talking points** are concise phrases or sentences (like short bullet points) that, when used, become succinct sound bites that are easy to incorporate in an interview.

Preparing Talking Points

During a broadcast interview, a spokesperson may be interviewed for a good length of time. However, most news segments will use only one or two points from that entire interview. Even 30-minute TV interviews end up being cut to just a few minutes of broadcast airtime. Speaking in talking points will help a spokesperson stay on message in a tight time frame with sound bites that make sense when heard.

When you write talking points, make sure each line is a complete thought, easy to say, and easy to understand. Avoid legalese, industry jargon, or acronyms to minimize misunderstandings.

Start by writing talking points on your **core** or **general key messages** as an organization. Those points usually include:

- The name of the organization and year it was established
- What the organization does
- Important details about its key services or products
- Important information about the founder or CEO
- Its mission, vision, and/or values
- How to learn more

PRO TIP

You can pull out talking points from any approved press release, statement, or media advisory available. Snippets of talking points also make great lines in a pitch email.

Anytime you have something new to say, draft a new set of talking points specifically on that topic. Our clients will have a set of core talking points about their organization that are **evergreen**—good to use any time of year. When something new, seasonal, or specific is coming, we write a specific set of talking points for those. Then the appropriate spokesperson reviews those talking points and memorizes them to use for interviews per topic.

Talking points are easy to memorize and review before a spokesperson starts an interview. For TV or Zoom-type interviews, you can review them right up until the camera starts recording. With radio, podcast, or phone interviews that don't include video, you can reference them during the interview. Just don't read them like a robot and sound like you don't know the material.

MEDIA TRAINING MUSTS

Media training is a common workshop request for PR professionals. As you're learning, media relations is a process to be managed from A to Z. Training spokespeople to perform well during media interviews is complex enough to warrant its own book. To keep this concise, here's a media training checklist to consider when you prepare your client or SME to be interviewed:

- Review and memorize talking points.
- Deliver your message slowly (most people go too fast).
- Help people understand with a relevant story.

- Offer context and untangle complex ideas.
- Get to the main point and fill in details as possible.
- Steer the conversation back on topic if needed.
- Know if a segment is live or recorded.
- Smile as appropriate and watch your nonverbals.
- Pause before answering and keep answers short.
- Assume you're always being recorded.
- Dress the part—wear a pressed logo top or solid-color shirt for interviews.
- Have hair and makeup done.
- Take virtual interviews as seriously as on-site interviews.
- Prepare a virtual "studio" with a microphone and flattering lighting.
- Never answer, "No comment."
- Ensure the reporter captures everything they need.
- Ask when/where the story will come out.
- Follow up with any missing information by the reporter's deadline.
- Review your coverage and document how to improve.

ADDRESSING AND FIXING MISTAKES

Always check each story after it is published *before* you share it with the client or organization. I've been in such a hurry that

I've been tempted to forward an online article to a client before reading it myself. I've learned that's not a smart move.

Just the other day, I was about to do that, but I stopped myself. *Let me just take a quick look,* I thought. Immediately, I saw that the reporter had misspelled the name of the spokesperson—whom the feature story was mostly about. The misspelled name was right in the center of the story headline!

What should've been an exciting moment for this spokesperson—a profile in their hometown newspaper—would quickly become an embarrassment if we didn't take action. It was too late to change the print newspaper, but we could get the online story fixed. What's online often lives longer anyway.

I contacted the reporter and politely asked if the misspelled name could be corrected in the headline and throughout the article. They appreciated how kind I was about the error and promised to correct it right away. Meanwhile, I knew the client was excited about the story and was looking out for it, so I emailed them to acknowledge it was published but included a misspelling that was being corrected. Things were soon set right, and everyone was happy. Whenever possible, jump on problems, and try to fix them before your boss or client points them out.

Journalists don't want to make mistakes that embarrass them or the people they interview. They will most likely fix a mistake in an online story as long as what is requested is based on facts, not your preferences. Don't ask for an edit because you don't like the wording or the tone of an article. You can ask for a fix whenever a number is misused, a name is misspelled, or something else inaccurate is included. For stories that were only in print or broadcast, correcting mistakes is more difficult. Forgive small mistakes in these mediums if they don't change the accuracy of the core story. A retraction can be made if it's factually necessary, but it's much harder to negotiate and is likely to be missed by the same audience members even if done.

Jeannette E. Garcia, a former PR professional-turned-business reporter at the time of our interview, agrees that changes should be based on accuracy. She stated that journalists often have to ask their editors for approval to make a change. That means you're asking an employee to tell their supervisor they made a mistake. Awkward! Try to get journalists the right information in the first place to avoid this uncomfortable experience.

If you handle error situations delicately, you can even deepen your relationship with the reporter. We're all humans, and we should act that way by extending grace when mistakes do occur. You're sure to make a mistake at some point, too.

BE HONEST AND ETHICAL

Creative thinking, critical thinking, and exceptional customer service are key responsibilities in a PR role. At times, you'll be providing as much service to journalists as you will to your own organizations. Keeping both parties happy will help you be the bridge-builder between them. Just never do anything unethical in pursuit of a story.

Since PR is the only communication area that secures earned media coverage, we should know our journalist colleagues better than anyone. For hardcore media relations specialists, they are the peanut butter to our jelly. To be a helpful source and journalist ally, support the sharing of accurate and timely information. If you follow a code of ethics like the PRSA code, you'll find PR ethics are similar to the journalist code of ethics. Be forthcoming, and never lie, exaggerate, or falsify information. It could get a journalist (and you) in deep trouble if they trust you enough to use the data you provide and it turns out to be incorrect. Even when you're dealing with a difficult news story, it's better to be truthful and fix problems than to try to cover them up.

WHEN TO HOLD A PRESS CONFERENCE

Too many leaders think holding a press conference is necessary for every news update they have to share. Less is more when sending out press releases, and you should be doubly cautious about holding a press conference. Before you even utter the words, do your research to know whether holding a press conference (a.k.a. news conference) is appropriate. Arranging and pitching a press conference event is taxing on everyone involved. It puts a ton of pressure on the PR pro to get journalists there, and breaking news can often redirect news stations at a moment's notice.

Here's when you should host a press conference:

1. When you need to get a message out to a large number of journalists/outlets at once and what you have to say is considered newsworthy. For example, updates on a mass shooting, warnings about an upcoming natural disaster, or the results of a high-stakes legal case.

2. When your news impacts a large number of people and it's considered a resource to share that news. For example, news on natural disaster relief, public health warnings, or an unexpected citywide boil water notice.

3. When there's a special milestone event occurring and it would be natural to share public remarks (must be newsworthy criteria). For example, a multimillion-dollar groundbreaking for an organization that serves a large number of people. Think major impact—a small business ribbon cutting is not consequential enough to host a press conference.

If your "news" doesn't meet these criteria, write a pitch instead, and share it with targeted journalists or outlets that cover the type of news you have to share. Targeted pitches are 95% of the media relations work we recommend and the coverage we earn for clients. This strategy works well and offers more flexibility in how and when interviews occur. Bad weather can derail a planned event, or a competing enticing story (larger press conference or breaking news) can redirect journalists who have even confirmed to attend.

Even if you're trying to get coverage for a specific event or press conference day, booking interviews leading up to that event or even after helps increase the likelihood of getting coverage. Don't hold back and limit the story opportunities to only the press conference in hopes of getting a large media turnout that day. I'd rather have some pre-event interviews happening so they can tease the upcoming event and there is some coverage running in case breaking news interferes. Most press conferences are scheduled around10:00 a.m. or 2:00 p.m., so even if there isn't breaking news, you're probably still competing with another organization hosting a news event during yours.

PRO TIP

Don't forget to assign someone to greet and escort any journalists who come on-site for an event or interview. You'll want to document who came, ensure they get the footage and interviews they need, and know they had a pleasant experience.

PITCHING SPANISH-LANGUAGE
OUTLETS AND PROS

The second-most commonly spoken language in the US is Spanish. It's pretty common around the globe, too. Are you including this large part of the market in your media relations efforts? In my experience, many PR pros don't.

There are many myths and misconceptions about working with Spanish-language outlets or journalists. As society becomes more multicultural, embracing multilingual needs will be increasingly important. Making an effort to include Spanish-language speakers is inclusive and socially responsible if you have news of importance to share in your area.

I began my PR career at a Hispanic boutique agency. Starting out, I didn't know the difference between what was called general market and Hispanic market media, but I soon learned about the divide. At a Hispanic or multicultural agency, you're going to focus on the unique cultural attributes and communication preferences of a niche audience. The biggest difference about working in Hispanic PR was deciphering when and how to use English or Spanish for writing, speaking, and pitching media.

I've surveyed Spanish-language journalists across the US, and they say the top mistake PR pros make when pitching a story idea to Spanish-language outlets is that they limit story ideas to *only* Hispanic or Latino topics. Think beyond stories that feature Hispanics or cultural holidays. Stories that are helpful or important to English-language audiences are *also* helpful to Spanish-language speakers, so include them both in your pitching.

Here's what you should know about pitching Spanish-language media:

- **Press materials:** Provide bilingual press materials if possible. Reporters are often bilingual, and some may even be more comfortable with English. Having materials in both languages allows for the best interpretation and gives reporters a running start on writing Spanish stories.
- **Content:** Offer equal-quality content in English and Spanish. If you can't supply a proper Spanish translation (Google Translate won't cut it), just send in English materials.
- **Translation:** If you do translate materials, be sure to **transculturate** or use a Spanish speaker who is familiar with your intended audience to ensure the Spanish is localized and interpreted to make sense as it is translated from English to Spanish.
- **Pitches:** Email pitches can be sent in English or in both languages.

- **Spokespeople:** Broadcast stations prefer to interview a Spanish-speaker but will work with an English-speaking spokesperson if needed. Ask what written publications may need for interviews, but it's often the same.
- **Media outreach:** Get to know these specific journalists, and learn about the freelancers who support their outlets. They often speak English and highly value relationships with sources.

Most cities have at least one Spanish-language television station, a couple of radio stations, and at minimum a bilingual print or online publication. Be sure to include these outlets in your media list and outreach.

Being proactive and as planful as possible when reaching out to English-language, Spanish-language, local, and beat journalists will make your media relations experience more positive. Like all relationships, the value will increase over time and with positive experiences. Media relations outreach may always be tough to do, but the results are worth it.

CHAPTER 3 TAKEAWAYS

To recap the essentials of this chapter, remember these main points and terms:

1. Media relations is challenging and should be managed proactively.
2. Consume the news to stay on top of trends and who is covering what beat.
3. Understand what is newsworthy, and try to become a source.

Important Terms:

- **Breaking news:** Incidents or announcements that happen unexpectedly and take priority in coverage (often tragic like a major car accident, celebrity death, or large fire).
- **Core/general key messages:** Timeless ways to describe an organization or subject in succinct points.
- **Evergreen:** Describing messages that are timeless or good to use throughout the year.
- **Newsworthy:** Information or story ideas deemed worthy of news coverage based on journalism criteria.
- **Pitch:** A concise message about a story opportunity and why it should be covered by a journalist.

- **Press conference:** An event created to share news with multiple media outlets at once.
- **Source:** A responsive, trustworthy resource to get information or story ideas from.
- **Story angles:** Multiple ways to approach or share one story topic.
- **Talking points:** Short, complete message points to cover during an interview.
- **Transculturate:** When a translator ensures language is localized for its intended audience and interpreted accurately when translated from one language to another.

PASS THE MIC 🎤:
VINCENT T. DAVIS

Award-winning *Express-News* columnist and feature writer Vincent T. Davis has been telling human interest stories for the paper since 1998. We've worked on stories together about non-profits, animals, seniors, and unsung heroes since 2005. His feel-good, heartwarming stories shine a light on extraordinary people in his coverage area.

Q. How do you identify a good PR "source"?

A. I can tell if a PR person is going to be a source with a gut feeling. Are they transactional and just trying to land their story? Or do they really understand what my beat is and pitch me ideas that I find interesting? When they reach out and share something they thought I'd like even when it doesn't benefit them, that's a real source.

CHAPTER 4

Planning Like a Pro

GROWING UP, I WAS A KID WHO LOVED TO EAT. MY PARENTS were struggling financially, so food was either scarce or too abundant. We rarely saw some of our favorite treats like sweetened cereal, so when we did, we chowed down. I was the middle child of five, and what I ate impacted me differently than my older brothers and younger sisters. By third grade, I had crossed some invisible line—from being seen as normal to being called fat. As a child, I probably picked up 10 pounds each year. I thought getting bigger was normal because kids grow each year. My weight snowballed despite my juvenile attempts to lose it. I tried walking, but we lived in a neighborhood where I couldn't go for a walk without being chased by a loose dog or hollered at by someone making fun of me. I made attempts to lose weight, but as a child, I couldn't yet comprehend some of the concepts in weight loss programs. Nor did I know how to stick to a plan, especially when the rest of my family could eat whatever they wanted. I was soon an obese college freshman. I didn't like how I looked or felt but didn't think I could change my circumstances. I had a watershed moment the summer of '99, my second summer at a photography job I had in college.

Leading up to the busy summer season, I was training new staff who had just joined the company. I showed them how to work the cameras, shared photography tips, and taught them how to use the cash registers. Soon after, the district managers began evaluating us for promotions. I expected to be promoted but was passed over for a new hire. I was furious. Why would they promote a new employee who I had just trained? I asked for a meeting with the managers to discuss why I had not gotten promoted.

"We didn't think you wanted it," said a department manager. She had a sad look on her face that made me think she didn't believe that.

I cried right there—tears of anger, frustration, and recognition. I felt in my heart that the problem might be my weight. At 19 years old, I was 100 pounds heavier than I am today. Whether it was the real reason or not, I believed that I was being judged based on my weight, and a part of me understood why. I was sweatier, looked more tired, and struggled to walk up the bleachers in a way that my thinner peers didn't. I probably didn't look like I could physically handle more work. I didn't look like the leader I felt like inside. As a child, I felt like a victim of my weight. My obesity seemed like a chronic illness I was born with and couldn't control. Up until then, I didn't think I had the power to change my life circumstances. Being passed over shook me awake.

That dismissal was a turning point for me. Speaking up did lead them to promote me to assistant manager alongside a friend of mine. I still wasn't able to manage things myself, but at least I'd been promoted. Then I realized how truly taxing that role was. I'd go in at 8:00 a.m. and sometimes leave as late as 2:00 a.m. the next day because the work was that challenging. That further compounded my weight issue because I was at work all day, and the meals available there were all I could eat. Despite all the walking I did, my body would store all the extra calories from the employee-discounted fries, chicken nuggets, and carrot cake that I ate. I soon realized that working in that situation was putting my health in a more precarious state.

Meanwhile, a college friend had joined a gym and was enjoying the spin classes. She invited me to a class, but I never had time to go because my schedule was so insane. I squeezed it in one evening and could see by the concerned looks from the people in the room that most of them probably thought I wouldn't make it through the class. At over 258 pounds, I cycled my way through each song. No one was going to tell me I couldn't do it! That class experience enlightened me. I realized that I was pursuing the wrong goal that summer. The better goal was to improve the quality of my life. No matter if it was right or wrong in my perception, I felt I was being held back and judged by my appearance. Plus, I could no longer ignore that this was not how I wanted to start my adult life. My professional and personal dreams were going to remain impossible if I kept doing the same things. My situation was going to get worse without a weight loss plan. I finally had the capacity I needed to take the steps to develop that plan and put it in motion. Over the next year, I shifted my mindset, researched healthy nutrition and exercise approaches, and put a plan in motion, and it changed the course of my life forever. From then on, I knew the power of creating a plan and proactively managing it. Being able to develop a plan and execute it is everything.

WHY MANY PROS DON'T PLAN

If plans are so great, why don't all PR pros develop them? Because they are hard to develop! I didn't say "write;" I said "develop" because creating a strategic PR plan is a process. It's not just writing ideas on paper that you staple and file in a drawer. A real plan must be used as a guide. What you put into the plan comes together in multiple steps. The content is dynamic because it comes to life in the hands of professionals and is iterated as needed when you implement the strategies and tactics. We implement, evaluate, and make changes until our goals are met.

As an in-house PR employee, I hardly ever had time to develop a campaign plan. I spent most of the day reacting to issues and way too much time in meetings to really think. I'd fight to guard my time so I could at least drop all my ideas onto a document, sort them, and share for approval. When I was an agency employee, we seemed so brilliant to clients because we had time to think and plan out campaigns. We'd research and brainstorm ideas until we could produce a document we were satisfied with. But still, lots of meetings happen in organizations. A big inspiration for me to start MVW Communications was that I was tired of being pressured to be strategic with little time to even be planful. If you're on a PR team now, I bet you feel the same way. Lack of time and experience often keeps professionals from creating communication, marketing, or PR plans. Running a project or campaign without a smart and preapproved plan can be about as fruitless as trying to lose weight without one. We can't get where we want to go without knowing the directions.

Planning is challenging, but it isn't a mysterious process. In fact, PRSA lays out a four-step process for planning anyone can follow. That four-step process isn't that hard to follow, but many pros don't know it exists, or they get overwhelmed in their day-to-day work and never put it in place. The four-step process also includes 10 different steps to include in your plan. You may not need or use every element, but it's good to know they exist and why. I'm going to break down these planning steps and show you how this approach can be done to benefit your work. Similar to my weight loss journey, a key part of developing a plan is making sure you're going after the right goal.

PRO TIP

Asking questions doesn't equal ignorance. Asking questions provides clarity.

THE RPIE PLANNING PROCESS

I've developed PR or communication plans for years in different roles and have seen planning approached in many ways. Every different organization, every supervisor, and every individual professional seems to plan their way. The PRSA **Research, Planning, Implementation, and Evaluation (RPIE)** planning process is the four-step method I learned about early in my career, though my understanding of it was so-so. As I advanced in PR and created more plans, I dug deeper into the details. The RPIE method has a lot of benefits, so it's my chosen method for planning.

It's really important when you're planning not to rush into naming all the tactics first. That's what everyone seems to want to do—just list out the PR activities like sending out a press release, sending out email marketing, or creating Facebook ads. That's the amateur way. Here's what many smart pros do.

Step 1: Research

First, you should do formative research to analyze the PR situation at that moment in time. Determine the business problem ("opportunity" in corporate-speak), define the communication goals, and then tackle all the other plan elements that come after. When you begin with research, you'll get an honest view of the situation and can be more certain about deciding what should go in your plan. Data doesn't lie, and it's a lot more objective than humans can be. Start with data collection.

The research step of the planning process is like the honeymoon phase. You're raring to go and can easily find information at your fingertips. With today's technology, there's absolutely no reason not to do research. There are two major types you can use: primary and secondary research.

Primary research is research that you conduct yourself. Examples of primary research include in-depth stakeholder interviews, original online surveys, content analysis, and more. Heck, even crowdsourcing using a Facebook or Twitter poll is primary research! Conducting surveys with tools like Survey Monkey, Google Forms, or social media is easier than ever before. Anytime you have a question during planning, find a way to ask it. Listening is the top tool I recommend for doing strategic, inclusive PR. Stakeholders want to give input and be heard. You can help them feel heard when you include them in your research. When they see you actually use one of their ideas, you've got both a solution and immediate buy-in!

There are many types of research. Here's a rundown of types I've seen used in the real world by PR pros.

Primary Research Types:

- **Focus groups:** Conducted with a trained facilitator. Can be costly in time or money.
- **Online surveys:** Easily done via SurveyMonkey, Google Forms, and more.
- **Intercept interviews:** Stopping people and asking them questions. Not always well received.
- **Mail survey:** Used more by municipalities or elected officials.
- **Telephone surveys:** Pricey and not as effective in current times.
- **In-depth interviews:** A favorite of mine for PR planning. Best to do with important members of an organization —not just top leaders but key program or service leaders as well.
- **Observations, visits, field reports:** Where pros experience the product, service, or program like a customer would. Document what issues you see, strengths to

capitalize on, and the user experience. You'll be able to share an outside perspective that can identify operational issues before they become PR issues.

- **Content or media analysis:** Review and objectively evaluate content that exists about the organization. You could analyze existing media coverage, social media channels, or websites to evaluate how the organization describes itself and how it's perceived to determine what needs to be updated.
- **Communications audit:** Review current marketing and PR materials to determine which materials are missing or need to be written in AP style.

Secondary research is information you gather from other sources. Someone else did the digging, and you pull out the data diamonds. Sometimes, secondary research may be the only type of research you have the time and budget for. At my firm, we do a combination of primary and secondary research in an efficient, low-budget way. For example, we may conduct a PR planning session with key leaders, interview users of the organization, conduct online surveys, and do online news coverage research.

PRO TIP

· ·

Websites are often neglected. Invest more time keeping up your website than social media because you own your website. Social media channels can change, go down, or disappear at any time.

At a minimum, we always conduct online research. We typically conduct an audit where we analyze the information, messaging, and chatter we find online about an organization. We also review the client's website and evaluate the user experience and the messaging. Is their content and essential information up to date? Is how they describe their program, services, mission, or values the same as it's written and shared on social media?

A standard of secondary research is online searches—like good ole Google. We like to search Google News to see what news articles have mentioned our clients in the last three years or which outlets have mentioned their top leaders. Sometimes, what you find is *not* good. It's best that you know what you're dealing with!

You can analyze all this information to determine public sentiment, messaging inconsistencies, how journalists perceive the brand, and more. As part of your analysis, you can ask:

- Where do we go from good to great?
- What may need a major overhaul?
- What may need to be addressed immediately?

Secondary Research Types:

- **Internet or social media research:** Google News, Ask the Public, Our World in Data, etc.
- **Research databases:** Lexis/Nexis, Pew Research Center, US Bureau of Labor Statistics, literature review, etc.

No matter the research type, the goal of all research is to systematically gather information that helps describe the current situation and determine where the organization needs to go next. Sometimes research helps us discover excellent ideas from across different parts of an organization or from its external stakeholders to incorporate in the plan. Other times, we discover the need to create a significant turning point and new messaging platform. For example, sometimes what we've discovered suggests the organization needs a rebrand to better tell the story of who they are today. That was the case for La Familia Cortez Restaurants.

From Party Plan to Rebrand

The first year I started my business, a premier events agency invited me to collaborate with them to develop a communication plan for their client's upcoming 75th anniversary.

If you've been to San Antonio, you've probably visited Mi Tierra Café. Mi Tierra is the "mother" of the now five restaurants the Cortez family owns and operates. The flagship restaurant is a 24/7 Tex-Mex food, bakery, and Mexican culture experience in one. I was the lead strategic communication planner on this project. To get started, I developed a research methodology that included a PR planning session with each of the three working generations of family members. We built a questionnaire for family members to review prior to their session and to share with family members who could not attend in person. During the planning sessions, the event company's CEO and I walked through each question and moderated an inclusive conversation so that all voices were heard.

> ## PRO TIP
>
> All information is important in the research phase—the good, the bad, and the awkward!

With that knowledge, we conducted online surveys with key external stakeholders of the restaurant. Including their most loyal customers' or partners' thoughts, ideas, and experiences showed their stakeholders that they were valued. Many offered interesting ideas on how Mi Tierra should celebrate its 75th anniversary.

We also did secondary research to review their websites, social media channels, past media coverage, and Yelp reviews. I reviewed all the data and created a situational analysis that illustrated a momentous opportunity. We could use the 75th anniversary year as a timely stage to reconnect the restaurants with locals, modernize the restaurants to today's working lunch needs, introduce the third generation of restaurant leadership as the second generation stepped down from daily operations, and connect the restaurants as a brand family. Our initial recommendation was to develop a corporate brand that unified the individual restaurants. Thus, MTC, Inc.—which was most closely aligned with Mi Tierra—was rebranded to La Familia Cortez Restaurants. This was one of many recommendations we felt confident making to the client because of the research that we'd conducted. The plan led to a successful campaign for the client and industry awards we could all be proud of.

PRO TIP

Consider offering to prepare a direct cost budget (advertising buys, media spend) once the items have been agreed upon by the client. You can waste a lot of time making a budget for tactics an organization hasn't even approved of.

Our own biases or assumptions about an organization and its needs should be put to the side during the research phase. Research is the foundation for any smart and effective PR plan. It's important to determine the organization's actual needs so you can set the right goal.

Step 2: Planning

A major benefit of having a plan is that it brings together all the important situational analysis information, messaging recommendations, and communication recommendations in one place. A plan is a guidebook for a campaign or project. In it, you'll cover what research has unearthed and what new messaging platform and strategies you suggest based on those insights. Most plans also list the targeted **publics** (PR speak for what most people think of as audiences) and share the PR strategies, tactics, and activities recommended. You can also include a basic timeline and a budget if direct cost recommendations are included.

PRO TIP

PR professionals don't always include all 10 steps in every written plan.

Understanding Critical Plan Components

PRSA recommends professionals use 10 steps to write a PR plan after the research phase. These 10 steps offer an organized way to include important aspects into a plan:

1. Overall PR goals
2. Key publics
3. Objectives for those publics
4. Strategies
5. Tactics
6. Activities
7. Evaluation
8. Materials
9. Budget
10. Timetable/timeline and task list

Including all 10 steps can seem excessive for some campaigns or overwhelming to read for some clients. A professional may not have the time to get through each piece before they need to jump into implementation (a.k.a. activation).

Here are the most critical, but often confused, parts of a PR plan:

1. Goals

Longer-term, broad, future statements of "being" or the overall outcome(s) of a campaign. The goal should explain the end result of what you want to achieve. In my experience, plans should have one or two goals.

Goal example: To be recognized as a national cultural strategy thought leader in PR.

2. Objectives

Objectives: Shorter-term, specific, measurable, actionable, realistic, and time-based (SMART) program effects that change opinion, attitudes, or behavior. Reaching your objectives helps you reach your goal. Write these *after* you complete your initial research. Plans typically include four to six objectives.

A good formula for writing objectives the APR way is **what** opinion, attitude, or behavior you want to achieve from specific publics; **how much** change you want; and **by when** you want to achieve that change. What's important here is to measure the *outcomes* versus *outputs*. Outputs are activities like distributing five press releases per month (don't do that) or posting five pieces of content a day. Measuring busy work doesn't matter.

PRO TIP

When people say someone is "strategic" or that a plan is a "strategic" plan, it means there's a thoughtful approach involved. *Strategies* are the approaches. *Strategic* is the intentional POV.

Outcome-Based Objective Examples:

- Increase downloads of my podcast by PR pros by 50% from 2021 to 2022.
- Garner five media interviews based on my expertise by a national PR trade publication by December 2023.
- Be hired by three national clients for strategic PR planning or advising based on my cultural or DEI specialty by December 31, 2023.

3. Strategies

Approach, road map, or general plan to reach the objectives. Each part of an integrated PR plan may require its own strategy (i.e., how you will approach social media, advertising, media relations, and content creation). You might create an overall messaging strategy for the campaign, have a complementary PR strategy based on that messaging strategy, and so on.

4. Tactics

Specific tools/vehicles for accomplishing a strategy. Most practitioners think about tactics first. For example, "Let's have an event!" or "Let's create an ad!"

Here's an infographic the MVW team created showing how they all relate:

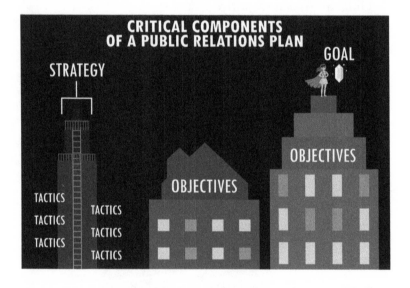

In this illustration, it's easy to see how tactics are like the steps of a strategy ladder. Using tactics that are part of a smart strategy can help you reach your objectives. Each objective, like these buildings, must be cleared (or hit). With each objective you overcome, you get closer to reaching the ultimate goal. For this superhero, it's about reaching that jewel. See how our superhero makes it to her goal with the help of each of these essential parts?

Understanding how each of these plan components works and relies on the others will help you build stronger, more measurable plans. Plus, you'll be well educated if you want to earn your APR. I earned my own APR in 2020. When I received my acceptance letter, it said there are only about 5,000 APR pros in the field with these credentials. Why? The process and test are challenging!

PRO TIP

The largest percentage of questions on the APR exam cover the RPIE model. Most working pros get confused between goals, objectives, strategies, and tactics. Knowing how they are defined by PRSA and how they work is helpful for passing that exam section.

Publics and Audiences

I'd never heard the term "publics" until I started studying for the APR exam. This was after working for 17 years in PR! If you're thinking about earning your APR, you should know that **publics** are people in a group who are somehow tied together or interdependent with particular organizations. These people have something in common and are in some sort of relationship with an organization.

Example: Freshman college students at the University of Texas.

While we may be more familiar with the term "audience" and think it means the same thing, in PR terms, publics are *different* from audiences. An **audience** is a group that may receive a message but otherwise lacks a relationship with each other or the sender. They're like a group of spectators or followers who do not have a common connection with one another. I think this is what the "general public" is most like when people use that phrase.

PRO TIP

The more specifically you can define your target publics, the more likely you are to connect with them.

Example: People from Texas.

No group of people is monolithic or completely the same, no matter how alike we may think they are. Even people from Texas don't all think the same! (No, I do not own a horse.)

Any audience can be segmented in many different ways and should be when today's world offers content for niche interests. Don't build a campaign for one vague group. The more specific you can be with describing your target publics, even down to creating a target buyer persona or avatar—like our marketing colleagues do—the more likely you are to craft messages and implement campaigns that resonate with them. It's a lot easier to find the right way to create a strategy to increase awareness with a target as precise as "women, age 25–30, with a bachelor's degree, who like cats and cooking" than when you're trying to connect with "women, age 18–55."

We'll talk more about tailoring for different segments of people in Chapter 6.

Step 3: Implementation

Implementation, or activation, is putting the plan elements into action. This is what most pros enjoy—doing the thing rather than planning the thing! Implementation is where you execute the plan components in the order they need to roll out. This will be a combination of actions the organization needs to take internally to get ready for an external PR campaign launch. For example, updating their website with current facts and figures, getting the top leader's professional headshot taken, or even fixing problems with their service that you discovered during the research phase. Clients often don't want to wait, and many want to jump straight to implementing all the tactics they've wanted to do. Guide them to fix internal needs first because scaling up before an organization is ready or shining a spotlight on outdated information is a PR no-no. It's our job to imagine how the dominoes may fall. Don't let an anxious boss or client pressure you to flip the switch that breaks their website or damages their reputation.

PRO TIP

If you're paying someone to help you, don't get in the way. The stakeholders who depend on you deserve better. Indecision is one barrier agency pros can work through, but a consultant is not being paid to play dodgeball with you.

The act of communicating is the heart of implementing a PR plan. Writing copy, editing materials, revising preexisting content, and pushing the approved messages through channels like the website, social media, video, newsletters, and pitch emails all happen in this third step of the process. A robust plan may take a year or more to implement. A shorter sprint of a campaign may be done in as little as weeks!

Let Others Help

To go fast, you'll need more skilled hands helping and smooth collaboration among professionals who are bringing the campaign to life. Sometimes, an agency tries to work with a client, and for reasons of ego, distrust, or even organizational territory, the client staff will sabotage their own PR plan! They don't respond quickly, they withhold information, or they confuse their PR consultants with passive-aggressive messages or actions. I've also seen this happen with professionals within the same department or in a department-versus-department scenario. Grow up, get along, and get to work!

Iterate As Needed

As you work the plan, monitor the positive, negative, or neutral results from the actions and messages you use. See what tweaks could be made to make the outcomes better. Allowing for some flexibility within your plans is a smart way to ensure they are successful. For example, I underpromise and overdeliver with all my objectives.

Say you write an objective like this: "Our goal is to earn or be coordinating up to five media stories focused on the campaign messaging in six months."

Just adding "or be coordinating" means the work can still be in progress by the end of the campaign. Sometimes getting a story in the news can take months. A great local feature story can take about three months from pitching the idea to seeing it in the paper. A national feature story I landed took eight months from conception to publication. So having some wiggle room in your plan is best, and managing expectations around earning media coverage should be something you do regularly.

If you are starting slowly and strategically, doing the work, reviewing the results, and then making iterations from there, you should be on your way toward meeting your plan objectives and ultimate goal. As you're working on the campaign, document how things are progressing because the notes will be helpful to make changes from or share with the client for iteration buy-in along the way. That documentation will also make your plan's final step and evaluation much easier.

Step 4: Evaluation

The evaluation part of a PR plan often trips up many professionals. This is the phase where we create a recap or report of how things went. Measuring our effectiveness is important, but measurement techniques aren't often taught to us before we start working in PR. Measurement is not even standardized by PR trade associations. PRSA has been working on identifying standard approaches for measuring the impact of PR, and they recently issued a broad set of measurement standards you can find online. Look that up if you want measurement ideas. For most campaigns, measuring with some tools and systematic approaches will yield a fine result.

The objectives you create for the plan will be what you primarily measure against. When you develop outcome-based objectives, you will measure changes in awareness, opinions, or behavior. The hardest and highest level of impact you can create is when you help change how people behave. But how will you know what impact you had if you don't measure it? As you evaluate your plan results, you'll be able to see what worked, what didn't, and ways you can improve next time. This can be especially beneficial because so many plans are made for recurring initiatives. If you are with an agency, noting how to improve for the next campaign is also a great way to leave the door open for a future engagement. All pros should work from insights they or their predecessors gained from implementing a past plan. Collecting data and measuring effectiveness helps make that possible.

The objectives offer a way to measure against the key performance indicators (KPIs) you decide on with your client or organization. Here's how you might measure objectives:

- Number of media coverage (a.k.a. hits/stories) related to the campaign
- An increase or change in website traffic
- An increase in website traffic to a specific webpage
- A change in social media engagement (likes/shares)
- A change in social media mentions
- An increase in social media followers

- A change in a target public's behavior (e.g., an increase in donations for a particular campaign)
- A change of opinion on a topic
- An increase in awareness of a certain topic

For a strategic communications plan that includes media relations, typical measurement includes:

- **Number of earned coverage hits:** How many stories earned on this campaign. Can be a mix of news hits and social media influencer hits (if they were unpaid mentions/stories).
- **Circulation:** The total number of copies distributed or the total number of "hard copies" sold of a given edition of a publication over a specific period of time (as opposed to read). The total number of actual readers is not the circulation number due to nonreaders and/or pass-along readership.
- **Impressions:** The number of people who might have had the opportunity to be exposed to a story that has appeared in the media.
- **Advertising value:** How much this piece of news coverage would have cost if you had paid for the spot.
- **Publicity value:** A combination of the estimated advertising rate times three due to the enhanced value of editorial coverage by a reputable outlet.

- **Reach:** The range of distribution/coverage that a communication product has.

PRO TIP

Use measurement tools to make your evaluation less complicated and more fair. I'll share my go-to measurement tools in Chapter 8.

THE DIFFERENCE A PLAN MAKES

One of the biggest benefits of developing a plan is that it reduces uncertainty for both PR pros and their stakeholders. When you walk through a planning process together, you've often had trust-building conversations that connect you at a deeper level with those you're working with. Often, we can make immediate improvements in our current communication strategy or even operational programs from gaps we find during the research phase. Or when things are busy and you get pulled away from the campaign, you can always go back to your plan and remember what you were *supposed* to be working on.

There's a well-told story about a professor who asks her students to put rocks, pebbles, and sand into one jar. When the students arrange them the right way—with the rocks first, then pebbles, and then sand—everything fits. Rocks, pebbles, and sand all have their hierarchy and place. Sometimes, I have to remind clients (and myself) to focus on the rocks and not worry about the shiny pebbles or sand just yet. A plan will help you focus on the rocks—prioritizing what needs to happen when to make real traction toward your goal.

MAKE TIME TO PLAN

Start planning at the beginning of anything new. Even if it's a small project, you can use at least a couple of the planning steps to get a simple POV memo written for approval. A POV memo is a concise, high-level summary of the current situation, the strategy you recommend based on the situation, a list of tactics recommended to bring the strategy to life, and the anticipated results from this approach. Sharing a one-to-two-page POV is a great way to get feedback on your approach and some leverage in case someone decides to say, "That's not what we wanted."

If you're working inside an organization, try to plan a minimum of six weeks before an important event. I recommend planning at least three months before implementation needs to happen, if possible. The bigger your team and the more financial resources you have, the faster you can bring a plan to life. For many of us, we have to do just about everything. Try to give yourself more time if that's the case. If you know you host an annual holiday fundraiser every year, then you should know the general timing of things, and you can get ahead of it with a plan. Remember, not every initiative requires a plan. Those that involve multiple steps, last for several months, or require multiple communication channels should be planned out. Once you do that hard work, it's a lot easier to update the plan for the next year and grow from there.

CHAPTER 4 TAKEAWAYS

To recap the essentials of this chapter, remember these main points and terms:

1. Developing strategic communication plans will elevate your work.
2. Use research to help guide your messaging and plan components.
3. Create measurable objectives that will help you evaluate your progress and reach your goal.

Important Terms:

- **Audience:** A group of people who may receive a message but otherwise lack a relationship with each other or the sender.

- **Goals:** Longer-term, broad, future statements of "being" or the overall outcome(s) of a campaign.
- **Objectives:** Shorter-term, specific, measurable, actionable, realistic, and time-based (SMART) program effects that change opinion, attitudes, or behavior.
- **Primary research:** Research that you conduct yourself.
- **Publics:** Groups of people who have something in common and are in some sort of relationship with an organization.
- **RPIE:** The four-step planning process recommended by PRSA.
- **Secondary research:** Information you gather from other sources.
- **Strategies:** The approach or road map needed to reach objectives.
- **Tactics:** Specific tools/vehicles for accomplishing a strategy.

PASS THE MIC 🎙:
MELISSA MONROE-YOUNG, APR

Melissa Monroe-Young, APR, was a business journalist for 15 years and has been in the PR field for almost the same amount of time. She co-founded the San Antonio Association of Black Journalists & Communication Professionals and is a member of several local organizations, including the San Antonio chapters of PRSA and The Links, Incorporated.

Q. What surprised you about transitioning from journalism to PR?

A. I made the transition when I realized the layoffs in my newsroom were coming faster than the new hires. I felt like I was on a slippery slope. As a working journalist who worked with PR professionals, I always felt like my skills would transfer easily to PR. I thought, *I can pitch to reporters and write press releases all day long. How hard is that?* I learned there was a lot I didn't know, such as strategic planning. I needed to learn how to write a PR plan with realistic objectives and, more importantly, how to evaluate it. That was part of what led me to earn my Accreditation in Public Relations.

CHAPTER 5

The Relationships You Need to Be Successful

ONE OF MY TOUGHEST JOBS ALMOST KILLED MY PROFESsional confidence. From the moment I started the role, I realized it wasn't what I was told it would be. I was at a corporation that I valued and wanted to grow with. To keep advancing, I took a new role in a fast-growing department so I could focus on **benefits communication**—a specialized employee communication role promoting health insurance benefits and programs offered to employees. Finally! An internal communication role where I could focus on creating content for channels we controlled (**owned** channels like the internal website, newsletters, publications, and such). I could take a break from the pressure to earn media coverage, and I'd be helping employees understand how to get and stay healthy. Piece of sugar-free cake, right? So wrong.

Soon after I moved into my cubicle, I was told there was a change of plans. Since I knew PR, I'd do the benefits communication and then take all the internal health and wellness initiatives and externalize those programs for customers. That meant reworking and creating programs, content, and external communication for customers while managing employee promotions and benefits communication. I was quickly overloaded with a job scope that had seemingly tripled in size. Because my new job was so demanding, it was hard to attend my typical PR or marketing industry luncheons. I made time however I could to stay connected with outside pros, though.

Most of the employees in my department were also overloaded with work and under pressure. I worked after hours to keep up, had less bandwidth for spending time with those I cared about, and couldn't do my best on projects because there were competing priorities. Keeping those outside relationships with industry peers helped validate my concerns about the situation and reminded me that I was a competent professional in a tough environment. Ultimately, maintaining my place on the PRSA board and attending events helped me be top of mind for an opportunity that could help me leave a role that was unsustainable for me.

One evening, at a joint marketing and PR industry mixer, I reconnected with a colleague named "John" who I hadn't seen in years. We had first met in 2003 when I was working at the Hispanic PR firm. The advertising agency John worked for at that time often collaborated with our PR shop, so I had interacted with him then. About a decade later, he was now a vice president at a large full-service PR agency. We had seen each other's life updates on social media but hadn't caught up beyond that. As we talked, John told me about a PR account supervisor role he was trying to fill.

"Do you know anyone who may be interested?" he asked me.

"I am," I said quickly and quietly.

"Really? I never thought you'd leave your job!"

"I wouldn't be a good PR person if you could tell I was unhappy from what I posted online. Right?" I said with a smile.

He agreed, and we set up an interview shortly after. It was a refreshing interview, with both the agency and me asking each other tough but important relationship questions. Would we work well together? Did I really know what I was getting into? Time would tell, but my current stress level was concerning. After a year and a half of trying to make it work, I didn't need any more time to prove that things would not change for the better.

PRO TIP

Sometimes you can *be* the change, and sometimes you have to *make* a change.

Within an hour after my interview at the PR agency, they called me and offered me the job. I was trusted and accepted quickly and easily! That trust was built on the prior experience John had with me at my first job years before then and how he had seen me conduct myself in person or online for years after. That relationship, not much beyond acquaintance level, helped me get out of one of the most stressful times in my life. He and I hadn't worked together at a company, yet that relationship did a lot to support my well-being. Right after I started at the agency, I became pregnant with my son. That was truly special because I had struggled with infertility for years. I can't help but think that the pregnancy was healthier because I was happier. Sometimes relationships outside of our immediate work circles can be the landing strips we need when our planes are almost on empty.

RELATIONSHIPS HAVE VALUE

Relationships mean everything in this business. Research shows that humans need relationships to be happy. In PR, relationships are our most valuable asset. It's the currency we exchange with one another, with our organizations, with reporters, and with all the constituents or stakeholders we support. Relationships can leapfrog people over problems and into opportunities. Building mutually beneficial relationships is our number-one job. For PR pros, those relationships are valuable to us and our organizations. If you're helpful to others, your relationships will come with you even when you leave an organization.

As much as we hear about artificial intelligence taking over communication tasks, it can't build human-to-human interpersonal relationships. A good PR pro keeps that top of mind. In my business, I value people before money or media hits. This doesn't make me the wealthiest business owner, but I enjoy a rich life. If you want to do great in PR, you're probably purpose-filled as well. If you're looking for your purpose, building relationships can help you find your way. Some jerks may work in PR for a while, but it's the kind-hearted, trustworthy people who make it through the long haul.

MANAGE RELATIONSHIPS WITH GRACE

Just the other day, I let a client who was having financial issues out of our contract months before it should have ended. Why would I do that? Spending more time together on a ship we knew was sinking wasn't good for them or for my team. There was no way our relationship would stay positive if we were not being paid on time and each month was tinged with tension from both parties. It's always best to leave on good, graceful terms and allow both parties to save face when possible. If you can, get out of no-win relationships sooner rather than later, but don't burn down the bridge while exiting. Try not to gossip or embarrass others, even when they do you wrong. With all the recording devices around, you can't ever really be sure where your comment will go or how the context will be rearranged.

JOIN TRADE ASSOCIATIONS

I've worked to build my personal brand separate from any organization I was employed with. To do that, I joined professional associations like PRSA at the very start of my career, and I have been involved as a contributing member ever since. When you do that, you get opportunities to work with other pros you may never be employed with, learn new skills that may be hard to learn on the job, or hear first about job or client leads. Some of the associations you should consider participating in are your local or national:

- American Advertising Federation
- American Marketing Association

- Hispanic Public Relations Society of America
- International Association of Business Communicators
- National Association of Black Journalists
- National Association of Hispanic Journalists
- National Diversity Council
- National School PR Association
- National Society of Professional Journalists
- Public Relations and Communications Association (PRCA Americas)
- Public Relations Society of America

Journalist, marketing, advertising, and diversity associations typically welcome PR pros. All organizations need allies, dues-paying members, and volunteers. Creating relationships across the communication industries can really pay off! Whenever you're a part of one of these groups, it's totally acceptable for you to ask questions to learn more.

When I was in the first year of my PR career, I received smart advice from my employer, who said I should join PRSA San Antonio. At the local level, I received the mentoring I never had as a college student. I was asked right away to join the board as their newsletter editor—something that terrified me. How in the world was I going to write a newsletter for PR pros when I didn't even know the AP style rules well? I probably would've stunk as a paid employee attempting this, but as a volunteer, the PRSA board was happy to work through my mistakes. The first time I met with the previous newsletter editor, she showed me how the newsletter was formatted and how to use the email marketing platform it was built in. In my draft newsletter copy, I had written out a long URL to a webpage members should know about. My predecessor showed me how to hyperlink the URL using Microsoft Word. I didn't even know how to create a hyperlink yet. Some working PR coordinator I was!

Whenever I volunteer, I always learn something or meet someone who benefits my career. I make new friends, peers, and mentors who connect me with organizations and media coverage opportunities and answer just about any PR or marketing question I have. It's important you build your own network, including trustworthy pros at every level of the field. My network has grown exponentially over time but only because of the effort I put into it. Building a network is not done by grabbing random business cards at a mixer. It's done by making connection points over time. The way you actually *serve* others is what will help you compound interest in your relationships. Start relationships and nurture them. Only ask for favors when you truly need them. If you're helping others, they'll be ready to help you in turn.

PRO TIP

Relationships matter, but shallow relationships will give you shallow support.

HELP OTHERS TO HELP YOURSELF

Help others by speaking to that class you're invited to, sharing a business opportunity, or being a job referral. I often think about helping others because of how others helped me. Reaching out is especially important if you're a person of color or if you're part of a historically disenfranchised or marginalized group. There are still not enough "seats at the table" in the C-suite when it comes to women, for example. So as leaders, let's make our own damn table and invite others to sit with us!

Ask yourself:

- How can I really help the community?
- How can I help others at work?
- How can I help on this board?
- How can I help the next generation?

Look out for other people. It will always pay dividends and not just in a business sense. Valuing others will help you gain authentic, supportive relationships that can buoy you through life's storms.

Networking is a process that everyone tries at some point. But many people forget about the importance of building and maintaining connections, especially outside of their workplace, until they have a need. As podcaster Jordan Harbinger says, "Dig the well before you're thirsty."

THERE'S POWER IN COLLABORATION

Keeping all the toys to yourself makes for a lonely kid. Likewise, keeping all the information or business to yourself can keep you from scaling projects and learning from other A players. Whether you are inside an organization, at an agency, or freelancing, find a way to team up strategically with other pros to keep yourself sharp. Hire support when it's possible to make sure you learn from experts in other fields.

My firm recently won several national and local PR and marketing awards for our campaigns. These campaigns were possible only because I hired other pros and collaborated with clients to make the most of all the expertise available.

As a business owner, I could choose to keep most of the work to myself. However, I know that two intelligent minds are better than one. Plus, if life happens or I'm committed elsewhere, team members can keep work moving forward. No star earns the stage all on their own.

The future demands we are agile and move with change quickly. You can scale up by working across departments or by hiring a consultant/agency when you need more brainpower. Then you can scale down to save money and adjust for a decreased work need. But you can't expand and retract yourself like a rubber band professionally too often and think you won't someday pop.

Collaboration makes us better. Tackling a problem, project, or personal goal as a team can increase the likelihood of success. Any task can be more efficient, smarter, and more fun if you pick the right partners. I've adopted this mindset since my school days and keep it a cornerstone of my business. Identify your most intelligent and reliable peers, colleagues, and mentors. Value them as your tribe, and stay connected to keep this roster top of mind. Collaborate as often as you can. Work-life balance improves, good karma increases, and your capacity to serve can increase with the additional resources.

ROR = ROI

Each experience someone has with you either builds or erodes your relationship. As my podcast producer Jennifer Navarrete says, "People don't passively experience us."

If 90% of success is simply showing up, how you "show up" really matters. No matter what you hear, business *is* personal because people like to do business with people they like. To calculate your **return on investment (ROI)** for making time for events and associations, you have to consider how you work to *earn* a **return on relationships (ROR).** This was a concept Jennifer and I discussed one day when marveling at how investing in relationships can pay off. For example, the ROI is what you get out of the effort or money you put into something. In the case of attending an event or conference, you'll increase the likelihood of benefitting from paying for the ticket and attending if you try to make a new professional relationship there. It's who you connect with that matters more than anything. New relationships can increase in value long after an event is over. But that's only if you try to create a win-win relationship that lives on beyond your first meeting. The relationships you build make networking a fruitful activity.

BUILD RELATIONSHIPS TO
BUILD YOUR CAREER

Investing in relationships is the only ROI strategy that has never failed me. Relationships are the key to any successful endeavor and vital to having a thriving career.

In PR, it's paramount that we foster strong, positive relationships with all types of individuals. It's what the profession is built on. From day one, I've had to push past fears and find ways to create rapport from scratch. PR pros must jump in the ring daily to befriend new journalists, inspire potential volunteers, or make a plan a reality in a matter of weeks (if we get that kind of lead time!). The only way I've been able to manage it all is by having the resources in human capital to call upon when needed.

My greatest ROI for my growth efforts is related to the ROR effort I've made to build and maintain positive relationships with others. That requires much more than a mechanical business card exchange with a stranger at a mixer. People who simply name-drop with an "it's who you know" mentality sometimes forget what's more important. It's really more about *what people know about you.* You can manage what they know by building a positive reputation from the work you do to help others achieve their goals.

Meeting new people can feel awkward. Here are five ways for you to authentically connect with others in ways that'll show a solid return:

1. **Get involved with a professional association.** Pay the dues and make that expense count by attending networking events like luncheons, mixers, or meetups. Introduce yourself, and learn about others. Find common professional interests to share as you get acquainted with new contacts. My colleagues at the local PRSA

chapter have been the mentors, friends, and lifelines I've depended on since the beginning of my career.

2. **Volunteer on the board or sign up for a committee.** You'll have to get involved for the best ROI. Use their professional volunteer opportunities to learn, try **stretch assignments** or new tasks beyond your comfort zone, or get to know pros you've never met.

3. **Give more than you take.** Share advice and job opportunities, or brainstorm with others who need support. You never know when you'll need theirs.

4. **Make friends with an industry veteran you admire.** Swap stories, tips, and contacts throughout your career. It'll be like mentoring without the formality that makes those opportunities so hard to come by.

5. **Champion others.** There are many women in PR, and women can be the worst about tooting their own horns. There's no reason we all can't applaud work well done. Celebrate others, and offer win-win, cross-promotional opportunities whenever you can. Everyone appreciates a champion, and those favors can return to you tenfold.

CULTURE PLAYS A ROLE

People from marginalized communities seem especially wired for building and maintaining relationships. Whether your cultural upbringing was focused on being connected or getting through life required interconnectedness, many of us who were brought up with collectivist values are super-connectors in this field.

In a **collectivist culture**, putting the needs of a group above oneself is valued. Decisions are often based on what's best for the group, common goals, and working together. Many people from Latino, Black, or Asian communities are brought up within a collectivist culture. Collaboration and supporting others are essential to collectivism. In the best cases, the family or group thrives together. In the worst cases, members may hold each other back as an individual tries to forge a different path.

In the *Latin Kings of Comedy*, comedian George Lopez tells a joke about how his grandma made fun of him when he got a promotion at his job. "Oh, Mr. Team Leader…" she teased when she found his department leader vest. Lopez says that instead of celebrating each other, Latinos give out a "you ain't shit balloon." I laughed because it was true. I winced because it was too true. I wrote this book because it's true. I'd rather encourage others to try to advance, no matter if they surpass me. While I value the advantages my collectivist culture has given me—like enabling me to naturally think of the greater good and build relationships—practicing individualistic cultural norms like assertiveness and independence have helped me, too.

At its core, PR seems built on collectivist cultural practices. PR pros work to create a mutually beneficial team dynamic. We help organizations build and maintain positive relations with the stakeholders they need and who need them. Different cultural practices can be an advantage to building relationships and working in PR when you consider how they may influence the publics you want to connect with. You may find you are able to build rapport faster with publics that are of your culture.

I've found that people from diverse backgrounds may need a trusted reference to encourage them to try something outside their familial norm. I call this my **invitation theory.** People from collectivist cultures appreciate when someone they trust invites them into a new venture and actively encourages them along the journey. To do well in PR, we have to understand the power of invitations and trusted referrals within cultural groups. Invitations and endorsements are best shared within a group and by a trusted source of information. That source's referral transfers trust as social proof from the sender to the opportunity they are promoting. For people from collectivist backgrounds, that source is often a family member, close friend, or mentor. As a PR practitioner, understanding this cultural dynamic can help you become or find that trusted adviser who can support your mission, message, or campaign.

Over time, you can develop a specialty in helping organizations that focus on serving people of your cultural background or one that you become an expert on. For example, my study of the Hispanic market began when I worked for a Hispanic PR agency and learned more about Hispanic cultural preferences. My own lived experiences were not representative enough to work from, but I noticed they helped with in-group credibility. My specialty emerged when I integrated my personal experiences with research I did on Hispanic and Latino communities. Their cultural preferences, practices, and what drives these communities to action are characteristics I learn more about each year. This has been important to me professionally and personally. The majority of the population of the city I live in identifies as Hispanic, so being able to connect with Hispanics as a core audience seemed like a smart strategy no matter which organization I worked with. Like me, the more you learn about a culture, the more likely you are to become a source of education for colleagues who don't have that expertise.

EQ > IQ

In PR, emotional intelligence often triumphs over intellectual or academic intelligence. It doesn't matter how much you know about a subject if you can't relate to the people you're trying to share that topic with. Are you able to read the room? Can you catch the vibe in the air, sense how people are feeling, and determine the environment? Are you walking into a room of excited fans or anxious foes? That level of emotional intelligence is measured as an **emotional quotient (EQ).**

Someone with strong emotional intelligence should be able to recognize, comprehend, and manage their own emotions. They are aware that emotions drive behaviors and can affect others, so they learn how to manage their own emotions. Then, they can recognize, interpret, and influence the emotions of other people. According to the Institute for Health and Human Potential, "it's a scientific fact that emotions precede thought. When emotions run high, they change the way our brains function...diminishing our cognitive abilities, decision-making powers, and even interpersonal skills." If we can manage our emotions and understand their role, we can be more successful in influencing the positive direction of how we and others behave.

Great PR pros work on their EQ, becoming more empathetic and aware of how what we do, or even don't do, makes a difference in our interactions. Being able to imagine the needs of your audience and what would resonate best with them takes more than just imagining. It takes research and caring. If you don't care about people, consider finding another line of work. PR is about relating to people, and if you won't do the work to get along with people, you won't do well.

Being emotionally intelligent means you should be able to perceive, assess, and manage emotions. That starts with your own. In this business, we deal with some chaotic situations. Every day is a little different. Even if you have a plan for the day, that plan may get scrapped when a crisis arises. Or, as we often say, when "there's a fire to put out."

Once, I was sitting in a conference room in this cool building waiting to meet with the owner about working together. I was in total admiration as I took in the stylish office ambiance. Then an *actual fire* broke out. You'd better believe my emergency preparedness, crisis communication, and EQ training helped! Some employees stood shocked, staring at the rising flames by the back window. Without really knowing the team, I yelled at them, "Grab your stuff, and let's go!" I kept a cool head, thought about safety first, and rallied people toward the door. I knew from experience that TV news cameras would soon be on the scene and prepped talking points from a safe distance while we watched the building burn down. It was truly heartbreaking to see that building go up in flames. Now, I am thankful for being able to quickly perceive what was going on, understand how people were feeling, and help manage the emotions involved so we could all live to see another day.

Work on your EQ for the rest of your career. If you become a PR leader, you're likely to be the guide through turbulent times and pressure-filled scenarios. Managing emotions is important when sharing sensitive information, handling a crisis situation, addressing a problem within an organization, or dealing with challenging relationships. Persevering through constant change and determining the path despite disruptions requires EQ. With a strong EQ, you can pick up on so many more signals than what people just say to you. Being in the people-first business, we need to understand how others are feeling and work *with* those feelings. If you proactively address a question or a feeling someone has before they even have to express it, it makes them confident in you as an adviser. For example, when it's raining outside, put out a quick message that the event is still happening, rain or shine. Don't wait until people ask. And don't wait until someone tells you that you're obtuse to work on your EQ. Start practicing that now, and ask for constructive feedback from pros you believe have a high EQ.

RELATIONSHIPS PROS NEED

Here's a starting checklist of the types of professional friends you should make and maintain throughout your career. These key relationships include:

- Mentors you can learn from
- Pros at your level
- New pros you can learn from
- Colleagues inside your organization
- Colleagues outside your organization
- Journalists
- Social media influencers and pros

- Digital marketing experts
- Community relations pros
- Marketing pros
- Advertising pros
- Graphic design pros
- Videographers
- Photographers
- Emergency preparedness pros
- Event planners
- Website developers
- Aspiring pros you can encourage to enter PR

Early in my career, my big, spinning Rolodex was a source of pride. It contained business cards for important contacts I should stay in contact with. While my contacts are now on my phone or LinkedIn, continuing to add to my list of valuable relationships will be a career-long goal. Make it your goal, too.

CHAPTER 5 TAKEAWAYS

To recap the essentials of this chapter, remember these main points and terms:

1. Relationships can leapfrog you over problems and into opportunities.

2. Our culture can help us connect with others in unique ways.
3. Serve others to build your network and learn new skills.

Important Terms:

- **Benefits communication:** A specialized employee communication role promoting health insurance benefits and programs.
- **Collectivist culture:** The cultural practice of putting the needs of a group before each individual in the group.
- **Emotional quotient (EQ):** The measured level of emotional intelligence one has.
- **Invitation theory:** People from diverse backgrounds may need encouragement from a trusted referral to try something they are not familiar with.
- **Networking:** Meeting or interacting with professionals to develop relationships.
- **Owned channels:** Communication channels an organization controls, such as their websites, newsletters, and publications.
- **Return on investment (ROI):** What you earn from putting time, money, or effort into something.
- **Return on relationship (ROR):** What you earn from investing in relationships.
- **Stretch assignments:** New skills, projects, or tasks that stretch your abilities.

PASS THE MIC 🎤:
MOON KIM

Moon Kim is a seasoned communications executive, team leader, and strategic counselor with over 16 years of experience leading corporate communications and brand-building campaigns. She is currently an Executive Vice President at M Booth, heading the corporate practice and a team of nearly 40 practitioners. She believes in asking tough questions, keeping an open mind, embracing changes, and taking risks. Outside of work, Moon loves to practice yoga (from which she tries to incorporate her learnings in order to be a patient and present mom of two), read about emerging trends that shape our lives, and experience NYC's rich cultural history and diversity.

Q. When should PR pros be concerned with networking?

A. Networking should never end, even when you have a job or you're a leader. I feel like I'm doing more networking now than at the start of my career! I network not only to find prospective clients but to identify talent to join our PR firm and connect with industry peers with whom I can exchange ideas and just relate to. We need to go beyond our traditional paths to find diverse talent who may have never considered PR but could be a great fit. Look beyond your personal network by participating in a panel discussion, reaching out to different people at organizations you admire or sectors you're interested in, and being willing to spend some time to introduce others to PR. I've been more active in my alumni networks and love to take calls with people who reach out to me. I find it's important to cultivate a network to really challenge me and help my agency find different types of talent.

CHAPTER 6

~

Use Tailoring to Serve Multicultural Needs

THERE'S AN OLD SAYING THAT BIRDS OF A FEATHER FLOCK together. Or, maybe your family told you, "Tell me who your friends are, and I'll tell you who you are." Those sayings mean people typically spend most of their time with others who are like them. Or, we can be influenced to change our behaviors based on who we're hanging out with.

This is the foundation of how culture influences our lives. **Culture** is the adopted set of behaviors we take on as part of a group. Our most dominant cultural practices often come from our families. My understanding of what it means to be Hispanic was formed by how my most influential family members demonstrated our heritage. The environment in which we were raised taught my siblings and me behaviors that we practiced during our formative years. As people grow and evolve over time, they can adopt other cultural practices that expand their preferred types of food, music, social interactions, rituals, and more.

As individuals, our cultural practices can help us find common ground with others. But if we hang out only with those most like us, our view of the world is limited. No matter our background, keeping our network focused on our in-group puts us at a disadvantage, especially as PR professionals. In fact, my success in this field is in part because of my interest in learning from all kinds of people. No one I knew from my inner circle had worked in PR before I started. Even today, people of color only represent about 24% of working PR pros. Not being willing to embrace guidance from white colleagues would have put me at a huge disadvantage. Connecting across the values we share with other individuals can transcend cultural differences. This is true for us both as professionals and when we work with diverse publics.

As people continue to become more diverse each generation, there's never been a stronger business case for embracing a diversity of thought, experiences, and backgrounds. Working with **cultural competence** is the foundation of building relationships with others. Having the ability to connect with people through their cultures and being able to shape an organization's culture will make you an exceptional PR practitioner. Chances are your own lived experiences can help you understand the importance of working with respect to different cultures.

AMERICANS HAVE CHANGED

In the United States alone, Americans are more multiracial than ever. According to the 2020 US Census, for the first time in history, the white population has declined. The face of America looks different, and that means the majority of Americans *are* different from what traditional marketing communications is set up for. If we try to focus PR campaigns on only the old "majority," our success will be compromised. Major growth happened in the Latino, Asian, and multiracial populations, and this growth is forecasted to continue.

The US increased by 22.7 million people since the previous census, and we're now over 331 million as a total population. Of that population growth, those who self-identified as Hispanic or Latino led that growth with a 23% increase. More information has come out in 2022 that shows there was an undercount in the Latino population in the 2020 Census. However you slice it, all stats are on-trend for whites to comprise *less than half* of the population in just over two decades. People of color now make up over 42% of the population and possibly more. In many instances, an increase in racial diversity means an increase in ethnic or cultural diversity. To practice effective PR now and in the future, it is a *must* to integrate PR with the best practices of DEI. Doing so is not as hard as it may seem.

Public Relations + Diversity, Equity, Inclusion Model

PR

DEI

Building Relationships

Ethical Advising

Marketing Communications

Relationships

Goodwill

Issues Management

Reputation Management

Sustainability

Appreciating/ Leveraging Differences

Providing Resources to Bridge Gaps

Welcoming and Including

©2022 Melissa Vela-Williamson

This model we created at MVW Communications shows how practicing PR in ways that support mutually beneficial relationships is in alignment with how DEI practices benefit society. When you look at the similarities in the middle of the PR and DEI circles, you can see how learning more about diversity, equity, and inclusion could benefit our work as PR professionals. Present and future PR practitioners should consider how these disciplines can support each other. Naturally, both fields are built on understanding and relating with people.

THE SIGNIFICANCE OF CULTURE

According to Merriam-Webster, culture is "the customary beliefs, social forms, and material traits of a racial, religious, or social group." It's also defined as "the characteristic features of everyday existence (such as diversions or a way of life) shared by people in a place or time."

Simply put, culture is a group's shared set of ways of experiencing life. Even animals have cultural norms. It's the basic way that we relate to each other and make sense of the world.

Culture can include our preferences for values, food/drink, music, entertainment, and use of language. People **assimilate** by absorbing family cultural norms as children and then **acculturate** by adopting new traits they admire as they mature and build external relationships. Someone with a high level of cultural competency is probably well educated and traveled. This leads to a broadening of perspectives and the introduction of other cultures. On the contrary, someone with limited opportunities may not have the same expanded global view. Diverse educational backgrounds also influence cultural practices. The education and experiences our target stakeholders have could determine their cultural practices as much as their ethnicity or gender.

Reaching the hearts of who we want to connect with starts with understanding their culture. Shared cultural norms are common ground to build relationships on. When people feel seen or understood, it's often because some cultural lever has been pulled.

For example, in South Texas, eating tamales during the holiday season is a common cultural practice across most of the region. Finding good tamales is a challenge because the tastiest are said to be homemade. Every season, people ask each other, "Where did you get these tamales?" Tales about the hunt for good tamales are plentiful from November through January. Looking for a cultural connection point like tamales—something favored by your target audience members—can be a great kick-start to a relationship.

TAILOR YOUR COMMUNICATION STRATEGIES

No group is monolithic, so no one PR approach will meet everyone's needs. The best way to relate to a diverse audience is to tailor PR strategies for connected segments of people. After you determine your target audience segments (or publics), get to know real people within those segments. Engaging with these stakeholders, asking for their input, and building programs, services, or offerings from their insights shows great respect for them. People want to engage with organizations and enjoy the chance to weigh in whenever possible. Why not start your work by listening? Organizations would benefit from working together with their target consumers to make products and services *with* their input instead of pushing something *on* them. Listening for insights will help you tailor your approach for the best possible cultural fit.

Tailoring your PR strategies and communication approach works hand in hand with cultural competency. Building PR plans with culture in mind means you understand what people value and express those values throughout parts of a campaign. Problems can arise when we don't consider how our communication or actions may be received by different groups.

PREVENT UNINTENDED ISSUES

The best way to prevent a crisis is by recognizing a crisis could happen. If a PR professional is observant enough to notice issues or cultural patterns emerging, they can forecast the likelihood of impact in their area.

For example, something that happens at the regional, national, or international level could have implications for your market. Recently, headlines about Black Lives Matter protests or an increase in asylum seekers at US borders should have caused PR pros to review if they were ready to address communication needs or challenges related to these issues.

One issue I see come up often is not planning with a people-first mindset. Any campaign—whether it is to launch a brand, raise money, or affect behavioral change—should be planned with the intended publics at the forefront. When you're considering how to tailor your strategies, create target avatars or personas that (respectfully) represent a member of each key segment group. Then, planning for their cultural preferences and needs is easier to do. Tailoring to that level of detail is the start of eliminating unintended blind spots.

PRO TIP

If you're ever asked to write DEI messaging, do a ton of research or hire an experienced DEI consultant to help. It's a specialized field full of blind spots for pros not trained in DEI program and communication strategy.

Not integrating communication campaigns across marketing, PR, social media, or advertising departments can also lead to blind spots. What insensitive advertisements have you seen lately? Those always make me think, "They probably didn't have a PR person look at that." Brands like Dove, Pepsi, and Gillette have received backlash from consumers for running what were deemed as racist, sexist, or tone-deaf ads. Many times, sharing concepts and asking for input across industry aisles helps us stop a problem internally before it launches publicly.

Every agency should have contractors who can help with planning if they don't employ pros across the communication aisles or pros with cultural expertise. Even independents or freelancers can team up to strategize and work together. This is especially true if you're creating a campaign for people of a cultural background that is different from the people on your planning team.

QUESTIONS TO ASK WHEN PLANNING

To put this tailoring methodology into practice, try asking some open-ended questions. For example, if you're creating an event or experience, evaluate:

- Which groups of people have been missing at your events?
- Does your organization or planning committee represent your target avatars?
- Are you speaking to values for this target group?
- Do you include representation of different types of people in your visuals?
- Which language(s) do your target segments prefer?
- Are prices tiered to attract different segments of consumers?

Look for the cultural gaps in your plans and activities. Be respectful when approaching this work, and involve your target consumers whenever possible. They always enlighten the process, and getting buy-in early in the process helps you create positive referral-based buzz when it's time to promote.

WHY TERMINOLOGY IS TOUCHY

The human brain is built to sort things. Since cave people times, we've been wired to determine which group we're a part of and which may cause us harm. While so much has evolved since then, our brains are still primed to categorize things (and people) as safe or unsafe. When we want to describe other people, our brains pull up those categories. The most common descriptions we may think of are often an individual's race, age, gender, or weight. While those descriptions may help us describe someone, those identifiers may not be what that person wishes to be aligned with. Terms, especially these kinds, can be touchy territory.

Try to give grace when people use terms you don't identify with. Perhaps it's our fundamental need to categorize others that's kicking in. Real bigotry aside, most people not familiar with cultural strategy or DEI practices will make a misstep. I've done it myself! Our own preferences and biases may shape how we feel about one specific term. So, how do you choose a term that's "right" when you do need to refer to a specific group of people?

The surest step forward for PR pros is to start with research. For example, the US Census Bureau category of "Hispanic or Latino" is not necessarily how everyone in those groups describes themselves. As PR professionals, we care about building relationships, which begins by working to understand others. Most of the identity terms we use in the English language were created in the past, and none will fit for every member of a group.

For example, terms used to describe Hispanic or Latino people are currently in hot debate. I grew up being told I was Hispanic, and as a kid, I thought anyone with brown hair was Hispanic. I learned I was wrong when a brown-haired little girl yelled in my face, "I am not Hispanic!" That taught me my first lesson about not making assumptions and telling people *what* they were. As I started to work in Hispanic PR, I learned how complex the ethnic terms for this cultural group are. Here's what I had to learn to be able to decide which term to use for what purpose when working with the Hispanic or Latino markets.

The term *Hispanic* originated in the 1970s when the US Census Bureau used it to categorize all people in the US whose backgrounds were in Spain or Spanish-speaking countries in Latin America. The term was associated with language rather than geography.

In the 1990s, as more people resisted the term *Hispanic* because of its strong connection with Spain, the word *Latino* emerged. By 1997, government publications had begun using the term, which referred to people with cultural ties to Latin America who didn't necessarily speak Spanish. Latino better accounted for mixed races as a category and is more associated with geography than language. By this measure, Brazilians who speak Portuguese are considered Latino.

Historically, a person in the US is considered Latino if they or their family have come from a Latin American country. People whose backgrounds are in Spanish-speaking countries, on the other hand, are considered Hispanic.

Studies by the Pew Research Center have shown the term *Hispanic* is more widely accepted by US Hispanics than *Latino*. This is surprising for many people because *Latino* was adopted by some groups because they didn't appreciate being labeled Hispanic and thought Latino was more inclusive.

From Hispanic to Latino came the term *Latina*, which is used to denote women whose backgrounds are in Latin American countries. In the Spanish language, Latino is a masculine noun, although it's meant to include both sexes. Latina became popular with women as an empowering reference.

In the early 2000s, *Latinx* made its way into the lexicon. It was said to be more inclusive by being gender-neutral. However, Latinx has not been widely embraced. In fact, the League of United Latin American Citizens (LULAC) made a public announcement that it would stop using the term in its official communications due to low awareness and acceptance of the term. The Pew Research Center found that less than a quarter of US Hispanics have heard of Latinx, and only 3% use it as of late 2021. This shows a big gulf between thinking and knowing when it comes to identity terms.

USE IDENTITY TERMS THOUGHTFULLY

Language is fluid, and the meaning of words can change over time. Which racial, gendered, or other identifying terms a person prefers comes down to their individual preference, the situation a term is used in, and how invested they are in that part of their identity. It's important to understand that it's impossible to be 100% right in regards to using identity terms. Being *technically right* and *culturally accepted* are two different things. You do want to show respect in your selection, though, as you strive to keep the majority within any group happy.

To determine the best term to use, research the group of people you need to describe. What term do they use in their own communication channels? How do the majority of those members refer to themselves when they describe their race or ethnicity? What does a cultural adviser, reputable academic, or community partner from that group have to say about that term?

Selecting racial or ethnic classifications is hard because they are poorly defined, and sentiment around them shifts. In most cases, the smartest approach to using terms is to use the two most acceptable terms interchangeably. Start by using resources like the Pew Research Center to identify which terms are most accepted by the majority of that group. The Pew Research Center nonpartisan fact tank conducts public opinion polls about all kinds of issues, attitudes, and trends shaping the world. Pew themselves use the terms Hispanic and Latino interchangeably in their communication to reference both groups. Since we don't always know the nationality of others, the approach of using two dominant terms interchangeably could be the most inclusive way to approach terminology.

HELP TELL DIVERSE STORIES

Think back to your history class days. Which races were reflected in the textbooks? The hard truth is that the stories we read weren't as multiracial as the makeup of society. As PR professionals, we have the power to change the stories represented in future books, movies, or even museums. The stories we tell through the content we create or media coverage we earn can be a part of making positive change.

I recently had the privilege of managing the PR and marketing for the HA Festival: The Art of Comedy during its second annual three-day comedy and film festival. The HA Comedy Festival is the world's largest Latino comedy festival, featuring over 40 comedians whose heritage spans Cuba, Peru, Puerto

Rico, Mexico, and more. Right away, I knew this was more than just an event-marketing campaign and that I should make that clear in the campaign messaging. Repositioning Latino talent as mainstream talent was the larger calling.

As a PR pro, consider how you can use the leverage PR pros have to lift the voices of others. What stories can you tell that go beyond who is typically heard about, profiled, or asked for an interview? What myths could you bust about marginalized groups through your work? Are there unsung heroes in your community, organization, or network who could be encouraged by a positive spotlight? We can use the platforms we have and relationships we build to create opportunities for others. Representation helps us understand who we are and what value we have in our society. For many people, representation can equal possibility. We can help increase the positive representation of a more multicultural society if we tell more stories about people that reflect that reality. Make it a point to tell more types of stories and include people who deserve a greater share of the legacy that leaves behind. Not only is that socially responsible, but it will help you better connect with the communities you serve.

TIPS TO IMPROVE INCLUSION

Some cultural differences in people from marginalized communities may keep them from being active in organized groups or feeling they have the agency (or right) to demand representation. They might be fighting for their place at leadership tables.

As PR practitioners, we have the power to influence change and can build opportunities across these barriers. Here are some tips to help improve inclusion:

1. **Invite contribution.** A respect for or fear of authority may silence marginalized voices. Make a special effort to invite diverse groups or individuals to get involved.

2. **Research your target publics, and communicate from there.** Use what you learn to pick the words, communication channels, and languages you use.

3. **Work extra hard to include women.** Women, particularly those from collectivist cultures, may have been brought up to be quiet or subservient to others. Make an extra effort to speak with older women who may not have the same agency as their more acculturated daughters.

4. **Look for a majority consensus.** Sometimes, small but vocal segments within a community try to speak for the group as a whole. This makes it even more important to conduct research to ensure you know what the majority of the group you want to work with actually feels and cares about.

Tailoring your approach will help you invite people into

conversations in ways that make them feel comfortable. Strategies like creating women-only focus groups, performing individual in-depth interviews, and slowly building trust with diverse groups or individuals may be needed.

CULTURAL OBSERVANCES

People enjoy sharing and learning about the history and practices of their own *and* different cultures. Connecting with people through cultural observances, workshops, and events can be a win if done well. To do this well as a PR pro, it's important to appreciate culture by being thoughtful in your planning. Do your research to learn how organizations have celebrated the kind of cultural month or event you want to have. What went right that you can learn from? What went horribly wrong? In many cases, **cultural appropriation** is said to have occurred when the use of a cultural icon, reference, or tradition is done in a disrespectful way. **Appreciation of culture** means there is a respectful sharing of information and inclusive participation by members of that group.

An article I read in *The Atlantic* by Jenni Avins and Quartz explored the do's and don'ts of cultural appropriation (which they argued isn't always bad). Here are ways I think we can evolve their tips for when PR pros plan cultural observances so we are appreciating culture, not appropriating it:

- Do include a subject matter expert in the planning, writing, or event activation. Consider inviting a relevant academic, nonprofit, or cultural consultant to participate.
- Don't include ethnic stereotypes or jokes.
- Do honor heritage and credit the source of artistry, food, music, or ideas.
- Don't use sacred artifacts as decorations or accessories.
- Don't hold an event about a cultural group without including members of the cultural group.

However you're trying to express appreciation, be sure it's authentic. Show you appreciate and respect the actual *people* as much as their culture. For example, an organization with a history of discrimination against women employees should correct their behaviors and show that correction publicly before holding a performative Women's History Month event.

BRIDGE DIFFERENCES WITH VALUES

The more "woke" you are in DEI and culture, the harder communicating can seem. What if your organization doesn't serve diverse groups particularly well? What if resources are scarce and you have just enough capacity to handle one type of communication approach? If you're not a DEI expert but you want to connect with people despite their demographics, try to speak to their unifying values.

Consumer behavior expert and author David Allison coined the term *Valuegraphics* to describe the shared values of people that can be used to influence and predict the behavior of people around the world. What people value can transcend demographics. Our values drive our behaviors and shape our cultural practices. Understanding what people value—their why—will help you speak to those values in your communications. If we start thinking more about what people care about versus how old they are, what race they are, or their gender, we could be closer to knowing how to influence behaviors that support our PR efforts. According to Allison's Valuegraphics 101 report, "Our values determine what we do." Values like togetherness (family, friends, and belonging) are a driving force shared around the world.

If togetherness is a top value, communication that shows that what we do brings people together could do well across different groups of people. Think about popular culture. Pop culture is enjoyed across communities because it unites people in a shared appreciation of something we're all exposed to. Pop culture is defined as the "people's culture"—a shared culture that predominates in a society at a certain point in time. Think about what was cool when you were a kid. What kind of clothes did you wear? What did you play with or wish you had to play with? What's "in" today? Chances are what you valued was similar to what your peers were excited about, despite their backgrounds. Tailoring your communication, programming, or services to segments of society is a great way to go deeper with brand relationships, but if you need to go broader, think about what strikes a common chord across shared values. I consider this approach a smart starting point for organizations of any size.

RESOURCES TO LEARN MORE

There's a lot to learn about DEI as a career field and more to learn about diversity-related language or inclusive communication practices. The Institute for Public Relations and the Public Relations Society of America both have resources online that are free to review:

- Search the Institute for Public Relations' Center for Diversity, Equity, and Inclusion for the latest DEI definitions, research reports, and webinars.
- Look up the Public Relations Society of America's } D&I Toolkit for diversity-related research, materials, applicable tools, and professional development opportunities.

While DEI may be a focus of its own, all pros should remember that working with cultural competence and learning how to be more inclusive with our communication practices can help us connect with more stakeholder groups. It's fairly easy to learn about cultural preferences, show appreciation for different cultures, and connect with multiple groups through shared values. Making this effort can be a big step toward honoring diversity, working toward inclusion, and shoring up equity deficiencies through your work as a PR pro.

CHAPTER 6 TAKEAWAYS

To recap the essentials of this chapter, remember these main points and terms:

1. People may be drawn to those they are similar to, but people are not all the same.
2. Increase your cultural competence to better connect with diverse stakeholders.
3. Use PR to help tell more diverse stories and help groups connect across similar values.

Important Terms:

- **Acculturate:** Adopting new customs while retaining traditions (adding to an identity).
- **Assimilate:** Absorbing cultural practices to integrate into a group (losing identity).

- **Cultural appreciation:** A respectful sharing of information and inclusive participation by members of a group.
- **Cultural appropriation:** The use of a cultural icon, reference, or tradition in a disrespectful way.
- **Cultural competence:** The ability to connect with people through their cultures.
- **Culture:** The adopted set of behaviors we take on as part of a group.
- **Valuegraphics:** A dataset of shared values that can be used to influence and predict the behavior of people around the world.

PASS THE MIC 🎙 :
MEREDITH LEJEUNE

Meredith LeJeune is the owner and lead consultant at Thought Bubble Communications. She's worked in PR for over 16 years in the multi-housing space, high-tech B2B, nonprofits, and multicultural communications. Meredith has worked from startups to global brands and is active with PR organizations like PRSA and the Black Public Relations Society New York chapters.

Q. What should pros who haven't worked with a multicultural community know or consider?

A. Minority communities are big on culture. It is what bonds us. Whether it's Asian, Hispanic, or Black, we all have our own subcultures and life experiences that resonate across the board. As a PR professional new to working with multicultural demographics, it is important to stay open. There is so much to learn. This doesn't mean you should absorb the culture and learn everything you need to learn, but it does mean you should understand that there are nuances. If there is an opportunity for you as a PR pro to help elevate the voice of an influencer in the community, you should make it your job to do so.

CHAPTER 7

~~~

Understanding Integrated Marketing Communication

I've never focused on just one discipline within PR during my career. As I shared in the first chapter, there are at least 13 major disciplines you can specialize in underneath the PR umbrella. In some organizations, especially private-sector companies, there may be separate departments for each communication area. I first realized this as a college intern in the marketing department at SeaWorld San Antonio. I was confused when I walked through the corporate office and saw that marketing and PR staff were in different areas. Why was that? Were they a tag team of some sort?

As a marketing intern, I learned a lot about promotions. We interns mostly attended public events with SeaWorld mascots or drove around custom Shamu Volkswagen bugs that were shaped like whales to attract attention. On a weekend morning, you might see me cruising around downtown and squirting water from the car's spout at families to inspire them to come to the park. It was fun, but at times I felt disconnected from our peers inside the park. At the corporate level, we marketing interns talked about what was happening at the park instead of creating what was happening at the park. We also didn't know how our work connected with the overall marketing or PR plan. During my time there, I didn't see the marketing team meet with the PR team. I did get to speak with a PR staff member and heard her explain the steps she used to issue a press release about the birth of a new baby beluga whale. But again, I didn't see how the different areas of communication worked together. I began to understand that advertising came from the marketing team but never saw how their plans were developed or how the ads were created.

At SeaWorld, it seemed that the advertising department created and managed all paid media: broadcast commercials, website ads, billboards, bus advertisements, etc. Marketing managed the creation and distribution of marketing materials (flyers, brochures, giveaways) and promotional events. Public relations seemed to focus on working with journalists (media relations) and managing community relations (mascot appearances for nonprofits and monetary or in-kind donation requests).

As an intern, I did not see all of the collaboration that I'm sure went on across the various communication departments. But throughout my career, I have seen and heard that too often, communication departments or different disciplines under the same area literally do work separately from each other. They sometimes don't integrate or work in tandem to make things happen. In my experience, that can come off as disjointed to stakeholders and is a waste of time and resources. It's like that old saying: When the left hand doesn't know what the right hand is doing, it's clear they aren't working together. In today's PR profession, we should understand how to tell a story to build relationships with others across different communication channels despite fabricated department lines. If a brand story isn't consistent, it's often perceived as untrustworthy. In an age of misinformation and "cancel culture," we shouldn't leave any room for distrust in our work.

INTEGRATE YOUR COMMUNICATION

Public relations pros are asked to do more with less every day. Many of us are one-man bands, having to be skilled in all aspects of the communication industry. PR pros need to be prepared to be proficient in PR and in the practice of **integrated marketing**

communications (IMC). IMC is the combination of communication activities designed to sell a product, service, or idea. For some professionals, PR is considered a part of marketing communication. However you see it, know that IMC is the term that illustrates when PR, marketing, advertising, social media management, and internal communication efforts are working together. In most cases, PR is about promoting positive relationships between organizations and the stakeholders they depend upon. Within IMC, PR is the heart that keeps all activities connected through creating goodwill. If you're reading this, you probably want to concentrate on PR. Knowing about the other parts of complementary communication areas *will* make you more effective at PR. No communication should happen in a silo, and understanding IMC as a PR pro will be helpful to you in many ways.

INTRODUCING THE PESO MODEL™

As someone who's worked in every major part of the communication field, I was excited when I learned about the PESO Model. This model is an integrated approach to communications that merges paid, earned, shared, and owned media types to establish the thought leadership, credibility, trust, and authority that fuel a brand's reputation. Finally, a framework that illustrates the synergy of how all these communication efforts could be working together. It's like a multifaceted Venn diagram that shows different parts of today's media landscape. The PESO Model officially launched in 2014 when the book *Spin Sucks* was published, but the process had been used by Gini Dietrich's agency, Arment Dietrich, years before that.

Sometimes you'll find yourself working in the profession without a specific term or model that defines your process clearly. It always felt wrong to me when communication departments were divided or didn't work together to develop their campaigns. Wouldn't they be smarter together? Or at least present a consistent message that could be tailored for their departments' individual communication channels. In my career, I often was the sole communicator for my employer, department, or program. That led me to organically manage not only PR but marketing, advertising, social media, and employee communications. From that experience, I learned to think about communication in a 360-degree approach. If I have a specific message, story, or announcement to make, I create a communication plan for how that will unfold across internal channels (employee or board members) and external channels (PR, marketing, advertising, social media, etc.)

PRO TIP

Always communicate with employees first. Too often, organizations announce something to the community but haven't told their employees the news. Employees can be brand ambassadors if you empower them with information. Or, they seem out of touch and can feel disenfranchised if they don't know what's going on.

I commend Gini for naming this communication integration strategy and giving us a tangible model that illustrates how communication should be expanded beyond earned and paid media. She advocates for a multidisciplined PR approach and embracing the nature of our changing industry. The PESO Model is a lens through which we can view integrated marketing. It's helpful to reference all the communication vehicles that can drive home a message using **paid** (advertising), **earned** (media relations), **shared** (social media), and **owned** (your organization's) media.

SEARCH ENGINE OPTIMIZATION
DOMAIN AUTHORITY
SERPS
VOICE SEARCH
E-A-T

MARKETING COMMUNICATIONS
INFLUENCER MARKETING
EXPERIENTIAL MARKETING
EVENT MARKETING

EARNED MEDIA
MEDIA RELATIONS
INFLUENCER RELATIONS
INVESTOR RELATIONS
BLOGGER RELATIONS
LINK BUILDING
WORD OF MOUTH

REPUTATION
CREDIBILITY
TRUST
THOUGHT LEADERSHIP
AUTHORITY

PAID MEDIA
SOCIAL MEDIA ADS
BOOSTED CONTENT
FAN ACQUISITION
LEAD GENERATOR
SPONSORED CONTENT
PAID PUBLISHING

COMMUNITY
COMMUNITY-BUILDING
ENGAGEMENT
 DETRACTORS
 LOYALISTS
 ADVOCATES
BRAND AMBASSADORS
USER-GENERATED
CONTENT

EARNED
MEDIA

PAID
MEDIA

SHARED
MEDIA

OWNED
MEDIA

LEAD GENERATION
EMAIL MARKETING
AFFILIATE MARKETING
INBOUND MARKETING
CONTESTS, QUIZZES

PARTNERSHIPS
CHARITY TIE-INS
COMMUNITY SERVICE
CO-BRANDING
CSR

OWNED MEDIA
CONTENT MARKETING
VIDEOS, WEBINARS
VISUAL CONTENT
AUDIO, PODCASTS
BRAND JOURNALISM
EMPLOYEE STORIES
CUSTOMER STORIES

DISTRIBUTION AND PROMOTION
CONTENT DISTRIBUTION
CONTENT CURATION
PUBLISHING PLATFORMS

SHARED MEDIA
ORGANIC SOCIAL
REVIEWS
SOCIAL FORUMS
SOCIAL MONITORING
PRIVATE SOCIAL
MEDIA-SHARING SITES

 SPINSUCKS

©2020 Spin Sucks

Created by Gini Dietrich of Spin Sucks.

171

This model offers a robust checklist for multiple ways you can communicate something. Many organizations think about media relations but forget to build partnerships or work with the community as part of their PR efforts. Or, they bet on media relations to shoulder the weight of their communication goal. Instead, diversifying their approach across paid tactics would help guarantee their messaging placement. You can sit down with your leader when planning and review the possible media types and tactics here. That's great because you'll look advanced in your knowledge of various communication types, and you can build a case for why what you communicate can't be carried by one approach alone. That's a huge relief for most PR pros who have undue pressure put on them to constantly earn media coverage to solve every communication challenge. Not everything is newsworthy!

Another helpful aspect of the PESO Model is that it includes the shared component. It is important that every communication professional understands that we do not "own" or really control what we put on our organization's social media pages. We share content with the real company owners of Facebook, Instagram, Twitter, and such. They let us add content for free on business pages, but they control how and when people see the content. Ultimately, they can decide to close their doors and shut down the channels. The shared component is the distinctive element of the PESO Model. Before I had seen this model, I was taught that social media was in the owned category. That didn't give social media the volatile characteristic it has in reality. Communicators who don't recognize that will learn quickly that social media tactics should now be under the paid category to guarantee the exposure and engagement it used to offer.

Every PR professional should understand the power of integration and its benefits. For an organization, having an integrated approach helps maintain a consistent brand story and messaging across multiple channels. For example, it looks fishy—or "sus," as my kids say—when a tagline is different on the organization's website, TV commercial, and social media channels. It's also a waste of time and resources. Why waste time rewriting something that's already been approved and may have brand equity? Or as often happens with communication segregation, why waste brainpower reworking a communication strategy that was proven successful in another department or PESO media type?

Here's how I think about communication integration and how it works well for organizations that have smaller budgets like small businesses, nonprofits, and educational organizations.

THINK 360° AROUND A MESSAGE

What's the story you're trying to tell? Nail that down and develop a plan. Then bring it to life across the most important parts of the paid, earned, shared, and owned communication options.

Determine which tactics must be used based on which channels your target publics use, the budget, and your capacity of time to execute them.

When I think about integrated marketing communication, I imagine a communication wheel like the illustration below. This communication wheel is how my company, MVW Communications, describes our 360-degree approach to planning. First, we develop a communication plan. We determine our goal, objectives, and core message. Then, we recommend how that message or campaign story should be communicated. Our plans always include PR strategies and tactics because thinking people-first and building relationships is always a smart approach. But if you look at this wheel, every spoke on it plays an important part.

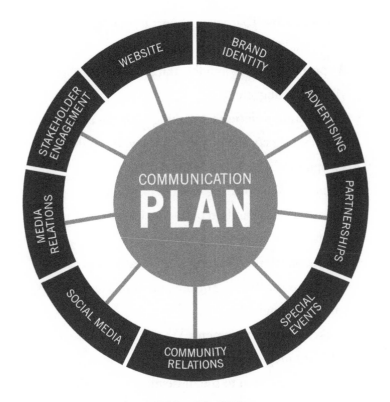

© 2022 Melissa Vela-Williamson

Let's imagine our plan included communicating the grand opening of a new museum. That museum should have:

- **A brand identity:** A name, logo, etc.
- **An advertising budget:** To guarantee announcement of the opening to targeted audiences.

- **Partnerships:** To garner support from organizations that could cross-promote the opening.
- **A special event:** Groundbreaking, hard-hat tours, ribbon cutting, etc.
- **Community relations:** Working with stakeholders like neighboring community members who could support or oppose the building of the museum.
- **Social media:** Creating organic/unpaid official pages on social media and preparing to advertise through the platforms to support special events, etc.
- **Media relations:** Pitching story ideas to journalists related to the opening of the museum, its leadership, and other angles.
- **Stakeholder engagement:** Working with museum advisory members, board members, or other individuals whose connection to the museum is influential.
- **Website:** Creating a website with up-to-date information on the museum, its leadership, how to donate to it, when it's opening, etc.

While the PESO Model offers a multitude of options, I've seen that sometimes that can be overwhelming to clients. Perhaps there's not time or budget to tackle all the tactics. Our integrated communication wheel focuses on the most impactful fundamentals of what has proven helpful in most campaign scenarios. Prioritizing which media types you use in which order is a strategic way to use communication types effectively. Typically, a client who is looking to leverage relationships and has a tight budget does well focusing on their communication channels in this order:

1. **Owned:** Always start with updating the media types that you control. Think of your website as your home base. Always keep the site current and aligned with the story you're telling. Don't launch a media relations campaign about a product if that product is not on your website. I've seen it happen! Also, be sure to include internal communication tactics in your owned strategy. Employees are too often forgotten and can be tremendous brand ambassadors for any initiative if they are well treated and informed.

2. **Shared:** You control the organic content you post on your social media channels but can't control how or when your content is seen. Update information here so that someone can find that info in a search, but don't think these channels alone can sustain your content and communication needs.

3. **Earned:** Pitch reporters a story idea if that idea is newsworthy (as defined in Chapter 3) but only *after* all the owned channels have been created or updated

with facts, figures, or information that backs up
that story.

4. **Paid:** Be prepared to spend some advertising dollars
to complement your storytelling in traditional media
areas and ensure your content is actually seen on social
media. The only way you can guarantee your message
is seen on social media is if you pay to boost posts or
create ad campaigns. Even a small budget of $250
can make a positive difference.

COLLABORATE ACROSS THE INDUSTRIES

No matter if you direct all the communication areas or not, you
should know which are available to you and how to prescribe
their use. The field you do most of your work in, or specialize
in, will naturally influence the way you put the tools to use. For
me, my PR POV, that people-first mindset, influences the way
I decide which media types we use in campaigns. I may not
use every type or tactic, but I know how and when they should
be used. Integrating a PR POV inspires collaboration across
departments and industry pros, which supports the development
of more relationships. An integrated team is powerful, and even
teams of two can work well. To even publish this book, I needed
to work with editors, beta readers, publishing professionals, and
more. Be an expert in your space, and let others be experts in

theirs. There's a combined strength in a diversity of skill sets, varying levels of experience, and different points of view.

If you work in an organization with distinct PR, marketing, or other communication departments:

- Become friendly with members from each department team. No matter how close-knit, busy, or even territorial they may be, all advertising, marketing, or corporate communication departments should be supportive of other departments in the organization. In many cases, it's their job to serve their internal customers (other departments) as well as external customers.

- Learn how things work to put in a request for assistance or who you need to work with to get the assistance you need. Figure out their timing requirements for requesting communication services.

- Don't just befriend the directors or the account management team. Make friends with the creatives—the graphic designers (a.k.a. art directors), project managers, traffic controllers, and other team members who make the projects happen. You never know whose help you'll need!

- Offer your expertise and support on their projects and serve them when possible to create win-win relationships.

- Start an internship program (or nurture the existing one), and help the next generation of communicators grow. Look for talent across PR, marketing, and business majors to assist you.

If you work in an agency:

- See above. Be especially nice to the creatives and advertising account managers.
- Help them understand what PR people "do."
- Offer your expertise, support, or shoulder to cry on when things get rough.
- Start an internship program (or nurture the existing one), and help the next generation of communicators grow. Look for talent across PR, marketing, and business majors to assist you.

If you're a solo practitioner/freelancer/independent:

- Find other independents to partner with. You'll need friends who are social media managers, graphic designers, photographers, videographers, and translators, as well as PR colleagues who can support you on PR accounts.
- Refer business to other pros, and ask them to refer you. Offer a referral fee or gift cards for clients you land in response to their referrals. Ask for the same.

- Start an internship and/or an apprenticeship program, and help the next generation grow. Look for talent across PR, marketing, and business majors to assist you.

INTEGRATE YOUR CAREER OPTIONS

Understanding integrated marketing communication is helpful to your career path, too. In the communication field, there are two categories of professionals: **generalists** and **specialists.** Most PR, marketing, or other communication professionals begin as generalists, meaning they do anything and everything near or related to their industry or field when asked. Many have plenty of stories to share about how they were thrown into tasks they weren't familiar with and had to sink or swim. Like a new swimmer, it's best to get familiar with the surface of the water before we dive in too deep.

Typically, as generalists, we have to coordinate or manage many aspects of communication, including PR programs, social media teams, or marketing activities. Or like me, you may have found yourself in a role where you were the only communicator and had to learn to do it all. As time passes and we gain more experience, professionals often discover their niche or specialty. That sweet spot is where we have proven results and a depth of knowledge, such as in event planning or media relations. Or, maybe your specialty is in managing PR for the tech industry. Hopefully, that specialty is also an area you're passionate about. When we're passionate about what we are good at, that's when our work really shines!

HOW A SPECIALTY IS DISCOVERED

Each professional should decide if or when they want to align themselves with a niche or specialty. To use my history as an example, in most of my traditional employment roles, I did a little bit of everything. I was the only communicator for a few of my organizations or departments, which meant I handled internal and external communication such as PR, community relations, benefits communication, media relations, and advertising. I even created or led corporate volunteer and DEI programs. I felt like I was all over the place professionally. Later, I discovered my broad experience didn't mean I was a jack-of-all-trades. That experience was called integrated marketing communications and was a specialty in PR! What seemed nonlinear became my differentiator—a unique skill set I have from my expansive duties over time.

By the time I started my boutique PR firm, MVW Communications, I felt that I could confidently say I was an integrated marketing specialist and embraced this vantage point as our 360-degree approach to communication. Even though PR is my main framework in communication, there are many ways that, through PR, we *are* marketing and communicating value with stakeholders. We do this when we share a positive message through social media channels, tell a story in collaboration with journalists, or even create content for owned channels like websites or podcasts. We live in a multichannel, content-on-demand world that requires us to be able to share one message in a multitude of ways.

WHEN TO DECLARE A SPECIALTY

It's been challenging to check one category or specialty box for my own personal brand as a communicator. Sometimes that felt limiting. I now know that I specialize in PR, integrated marketing communications, and Hispanic/Latino cultural or DEI strategy. My firm has a focus on serving nonprofits, education organizations, and corporations that want to do social good.

Even if you don't want to declare a certain discipline as a specialty, perhaps your business sector requires specialization. Depending on what sector you work in, you will find the terminology and regulations may be different and critical for you to know. For instance, what you should write in a press release for a public company is very different from what you may put in a press release for a private company or nonprofit organization. Also, many PR pros in governmental affairs have to register as lobbyists because they are seen as promoting issues or causes on behalf of the institution. Once you decide on a specialty, search online for niche trade associations, nonprofits, or reputable publications related to that specialty. You can reference them to learn more about specific terms or regulations that pertain to that specialty. Even better, get formal training or earn a certification in that specialty. It'll level you up as a pro and help distinguish your specialization. Don't forget you can always ask an experienced specialist in that area for guidance on educational resources.

For example, when I started working in DEI, I read *The International Diversity & Inclusion Lexicon*, which helped me learn diversity terms, concepts, and regulations I wasn't familiar with. Then, I joined the Texas Diversity Council to meet working professionals and attend their industry events. Now that I'm looking to further integrate DEI with PR, I'm studying for my certification as a diversity professional through the Institute for Diversity Certification. Their textbook alone has shown me many concepts, terms, models, and legal aspects of DEI that I wouldn't have known simply by working in PR.

PROS AND CONS OF SPECIALIZING

What seems to be most beneficial in our fluid world is that we have *generalist capabilities* and *an integrated mindset*. That means that you could specialize in a certain topic or category, but you should have an understanding of the other communication areas that benefit your work. Learn enough about social media and marketing elements, advertising strategies, or PR principles so that you can advise your organization or client when to incorporate those parts of the field. The evolution of the PR profession demands we keep learning.

FLEXIBILITY > SPECIALTY

Because I'm passionate about culture, education, and nonprofits, I've gone deeper in these categories throughout my career where I could apply any of the communication areas as strategic approaches to issues. However, I've been careful to keep myself from being labeled or known as "only" good at this or that. Focusing on a specialty or niche can be lucrative—they say the riches are in the niches—but be careful not to pigeonhole yourself into a space so tight that you can't easily transfer to another department or role if needed. If the COVID-19 pandemic has taught us anything, it's that we have to be flexible and understand that jobs or even industries can change quickly.

How do you become nimbler if you practiced in one sector or discipline most of your career? Or, if you don't have any experience at all? Find places you can volunteer in different media areas, or take classes to expand your skill set. Or, help a small business owner and support their growth while you practice something new. Taking a free online course and investing in a professional certification are smart options, too.

Strategic communication doesn't happen in only one specialty area. Learning how to work smoothly across departments or to keep partner experts at hand will make you especially valuable to any client or organization. It will help you be more agile and career-resilient as our society shifts, too.

CHAPTER 7 TAKEAWAYS

To recap the essentials of this chapter, remember these main points and terms:

1. Integrate communication media types to maximize your communication efforts.
2. PR pros can use the PESO Model or a simplified version to describe and practice integrated marketing communication.
3. Specialties can be developed over time but come with pros and cons.

Important Terms:

- **Generalist:** A professional who does a little bit of everything related to their profession.

- **Integrated marketing communications (IMC):**
  The combination of communication activities designed
  to sell a product, service, or idea.
- **Paid versus earned versus shared versus owned media:**
  Advertising (paid for inclusion), media relations (earned
  unpaid/publicity inclusion), social media (you share the
  content), your channels (you own/control the media
  channels).
- **PESO Model:** An integrated approach to communications that merges paid, earned, shared, and owned media
  types created by Gini Dietrich and *Spin Sucks*.
- **Specialist:** A professional who focuses on a certain
  discipline in PR.

PASS THE MIC 🎤:
GINI DIETRICH

Gini Dietrich is the founder and CEO of *Spin Sucks* blog, host of the *Spin Sucks* podcast, and author of *Spin Sucks* (the book). She is the creator of the PESO Model™ and has crafted a certification for the PESO Model™ in partnership with Syracuse University. Spin Sucks is a leading source for modern PR training, trends, and insights through the Spin Sucks blog, online community, book and podcast.

Q. What part of integrated marketing communication program execution do pros get wrong?

A. There are two things communicators get wrong. One is the defensiveness that comes with working with marketing. It's probably human nature, but I see a lot of people sort of put their arms around what they manage. They're not willing to collaborate. The second is that marketing professionals tend to focus on one thing and one thing only. We hear it often in the Spin Sucks community—how do I invest in my own professional development? As pros, we have to focus on ourselves, too. We have to make time to invest in our own professional development so we don't get stuck professionally.

CHAPTER 8

~

Building Your
PR Toolkit

When I started working in PR, my primary PR tool was Yahoo search. Then my boss introduced me to Google. Game-changer. "Google it" is now the first thing that comes to mind when I don't know something. Google remains an important tool, but there are many more tools PR pros should be familiar with.

I didn't realize how empty my PR toolkit was until I had to create my first **media recap.** Measuring media story coverage value and compiling clips were probably the most laborious parts of my agency job. After a media outreach campaign, we used to track down articles in print publications and cut them all out to save in a binder. Then, we measured their column length and width and used those measurements to figure out the advertising cost for what each size story would have cost if we had purchased that size ad. Then we'd multiply that number times three to calculate the PR value (a story's believability compared to an ad). What a mathematical nightmare.

Finding broadcast stories was a whole other process. One that included actually tuning in to try to catch a story! Online stories were easier to find but harder to measure. For all the mediums, we'd get the advertising rates by requesting media kits from each outlet's advertising sales reps. That meant we'd start getting hounded to purchase advertising for clients. Measuring the value of coverage and compiling it all in one place was a complicated, time-sucking mess.

There weren't fancy tools for measurement or finding these metrics back then. Or maybe the agencies I worked with didn't know about them or have the budget to purchase them. For your career, you should know what options are out there so you can request them or invest in them yourself. Having the right tools on hand will make your job easier and your approach more systematic. PR measurement has become more important than ever, and having a toolkit can help you better illustrate the impact your work has. We'll go through some of my favorite PR tools in this chapter. Many more exist, so test products and add what you like to your toolkit as you advance throughout your career.

PRO TIP

If you like a journalist's article, you can send them an email telling them so to start your relationship on a positive note.

PURCHASE PRINT SUBSCRIPTIONS

Way too often, PR pros forget the importance of simply reading the daily newspaper or watching broadcast news themselves. Your organization should have a paid subscription to every major newspaper or magazine that you frequently pitch story ideas to. There are two reasons for that. The first is that you want to be able to monitor what kinds of stories they're reporting on and get to know what the journalists in your focus area like to write stories about.

The second is that you'll learn something in every newspaper or magazine you actually read. You'll find contact list information, such as emails or phone numbers. You'll learn about changing editors or news reporters, or you'll get a hint of the next publication's editorial theme. Sometimes you'll see awards submission opportunities or upcoming events that will benefit you or your organization. It's rare that I don't learn a new piece of information or come up with a new story angle every time I read print news.

For most PR pros, your main media outreach targets will be news outlets where your organization does business. If you do a lot of regional, national, or international pitching, make sure you have subscriptions to relevant outlets there. It comes off as tacky when PR pros say they don't have a subscription to a mainstream outlet like the daily newspaper or the local business magazine. It's a business expense worth having because you don't want to ask journalists to help you view an article behind their paywall. Or be unable to share it with your client because your agency doesn't have a subscription. Encourage organizations and clients you're connected with to purchase subscriptions or consider advertising. We want journalists to work with us on stories, but they can't do that if their newsrooms shut down due to financial troubles. The newsrooms have gotten leaner and the **newshole,** the area of print journalism available for editorial stories, has shrunken because of that. Consider subscriptions as a tool for your toolkit, and maintain paid subscriptions to the news outlets you rely on. Many times, a digital-only subscription has a very nominal fee. If a tool makes you a better professional, it's often worth the money. Even if you have to pay for a subscription yourself, that subscription can move on with you if you take another job.

MONITORING TOOLS

Learn to monitor media outlets for earned coverage and to monitor social media channels for brand mentions as part of your PR work. Doing so supports a well-balanced brand reputation strategy. Offensively, you'll be aware of the sentiment around your organization's brand, be better equipped to catch media coverage you helped secure, and decipher which of your angles are most newsworthy to journalists. Defensively, it's best to mitigate an issue before it spins out of control. Being aware of what's being said or asked about the brand is important to catch emerging issues. Even if the chatter is positive, you can pick up on keywords, messages, or even news story angles based on what people are sharing and talking about.

On the news media side, there are times when you should hire a monitoring company to monitor the TV and radio newscasts to catch mentions of your organization or client. Tools like Aircheck, which records television and radio news, can pull up any mentions that come up through a keyword search. I find this valuable when the stakes are high, such as during a crisis or leading into a press event. For example, if we have a press conference happening, we will want to monitor coverage to catch any mentions. Sometimes TV news will produce a story or mention without ever telling us! That happens a lot when you get mentions leading up to a big event. Sometimes journalists will mention an upcoming event in the morning or lifestyle news show banter. There's no way you'd be able to catch mentions like these on your own unless you sat and watched every news broadcast all day long. Plus, reporting services will give you metrics, such as the advertising value of that segment, publicity value, number of Nielsen TV watchers, number of radio listeners, and more. It makes putting together a media recap a lot easier and more accurate.

Here are some tools that can help you find media coverage and social media chatter.

Free tools:

- Google Alerts
- Talkwalker Alerts
- Google searches
- Mention

Paid tools:

- Burrelles
- AirCheck
- TVEyes
- Cision
- Critical Mention
- Brandwatch

MEDIA RECAP CREATION TOOLS

Putting together media recaps is easier these days because of tools. After you gather the articles (stories/clips), take screenshots of TV/radio broadcast stories, and pull together all the metrics you can source, it's time to compile the data and add up the numbers. This can be done in a spreadsheet, for which someone does all the calculations by hand and enters in all the information like I used to. Or even better, tools like Coveragebook or Nectarize can help you find some of the measurement numbers you need and compile the recap for you!

PRO TIP

Systematize everything you can for efficiency and fairness when creating earned coverage/media recaps. Coveragebook is my main recap-building platform, and I use monitoring tools to gather the stories and broadcast metrics to fill measurement gaps. No one tool seems to do it all (well).

Common metrics included in earned coverage recaps are:

- Total number of clips/stories/pieces of coverage

- Online readership by article or website
- Print readership or circulation
- Estimated views: How many people were estimated to have viewed your content
- Impressions: How many people were shown your message
- Advertising value: What it would cost if you had purchased that advertising space or time
- Publicity or editorial value: The value of what the public perceives as a third-party endorsement from journalists
- Number of TV viewers
- Number of radio listeners
- Number of email/online/other subscribers
- Social media reach
- Social media engagement (likes, shares

MEDIA LIST CREATION TOOLS

Creating a media list or updating the one you have is an important part of media relations. To be able to do media outreach, you need to have all your contact information together. You can pull that together using a paid tool like those below. Or make one yourself by going to each media outlet's website, finding the contact information for editorial staff, and compiling the information using a simple spreadsheet. Media lists are only as good as their last update, and journalists find new jobs often. Some of them are now in PR. Maybe that's you! Keep updating your media list. A media list that's accurate and contains contacts you can pitch stories to is a valuable tool.

Free tools:

- Each media outlet's website
- Twitter: Journalists hang out there, and many display their email addresses
- Google Sheets

Paid tools:

- Cision
- Muck Rack
- Agility PR

PRESS KIT ELEMENTS

Being a strong writer and editor is a must in PR. Effective PR professionals specialize in writing materials in AP style that share factual information, highlight essential points, and answer typical questions before a reporter needs to ask them.

PRO TIP

Sometimes you have to adjust to another writing style so *you* don't look wrong! "Flyer" is actually written as "flier" in AP style. I once got in a senseless disagreement with a co-worker over the correct way to write that term. I was right, but the word looked wrong. Since most people use "flyer," I use that spelling most often now.

Also known as a media kit, a **press kit** contains written materials journalists use to quickly gather data. Even the smallest of organizations should have media-friendly materials. For instance, when I started a job at a nonprofit, one of the first things I did was audit the marketing materials they had on hand. What I saw was a lot of flyers. Flyers are great for marketing but don't often include essential facts journalists need. By then, I had some PR agency experience and knew the value of a good press kit. I set about creating one right away. Today, I audit each client during onboarding to see what press kit they do (or don't) have. Creating or updating an organization's press kit is a sound starting point for your PR efforts.

A full press kit includes:

- **Fact sheet(s):** A one-page document that overviews the organization or topic.
- **Top leader(s) or spokesperson(s) bio:** A short and long version is helpful.
- **Top leader(s) or spokesperson(s) headshot:** Must be high resolution and flattering.
- **Boilerplate:** One paragraph that gives an overview of the organization and where to learn more about it.
- **Backgrounder:** Two or more pages of facts and information on an organization or topic.
- **Press/news/media release:** A narrative way to summarize an announcement or happening. They are written in past tense if a release is shared after a media alert has been distributed about a special event. They are written in present tense if the release is a stand-alone announcement.
- **Media alert/media advisory/request for coverage:** An invitation to the media to cover a special event or press event.
- **Talking points:** Short, complete points to cover during an interview.
- **Cloud storage folder of visual assets:** Photos, logos (JPG or PNG format), and video B-roll footage that journalists can use.

The elements of a press kit are tools and should be handed out as such—the right tool for the right job. Keep them updated, and make sure the organization preapproves them. Have them ready to go at a moment's notice. I keep press kit documents in a cloud folder so I can send them from my phone as needed.

TWO ESSENTIAL MEDIA MATERIALS

Resources are often limited in PR. Sometimes there's not enough time to develop a complete press kit. If you need to move fast, two pieces of PR materials can cover most of your needs:

1. Media advisory:
   - Also known as a media alert or a request for coverage.
   - Includes concise info that's an invitation for journalists to see/attend a special happening.
   - Format should include who, what, when, where, why and visuals.
   - Include media contact info and any special instructions on parking or advance registration (for more exclusive press events).
2. Press release:
   - Also known as a media release.
   - Includes background details in a narrative format.
   - Written in past tense.

- Can include quotes from the lead organization and involved stakeholders.
- Good tool to use for follow-up.
- Share as a supplement to media advisories during or after the event.
- May be the only PR tool used/needed if there is not an event to invite media to cover.

Journalists have told me that those two written materials are all they really need. Write them in AP style, and keep them error-free. Make sure to include newsworthy criteria information within the copy as you write them. You can find examples of how to a format either of these materials by searching online. For example, "AP style press release template" brings up some helpful options.

PRO TIP

Learn how to write them, but don't overthink media materials. Your relationships and understanding of news matters more. I once created an award-winning media relations campaign from just talking points because time was short!

PROVIDING VISUAL ASSETS

Reporters are fewer in number and busier than ever. While it used to be considered rude to offer photos and videos to a reporter, it's now considered helpful. Try to prepare B-roll and photos to accompany any pitch, alert, or press release you send out. What you can create with smartphones works well enough for most needs.

Video and photo specifics:

- Always shoot video (B-roll) in horizontal/landscape mode to fill up a TV screen.
- For a voiceover (VO), make sure the narrator is wearing a microphone, and keep the VO to 15–20 seconds.
- For video and sound on tape (VSOT), keep it under 30 seconds.
- For interview soundbites, keep them around 15–20 seconds.
- Photos should be shot in horizontal and vertical options and be high resolution.
- Make sure you have signed media releases or permission from all people in photos.
- Include copyright credit information, such as, "Courtesy of MVW Communications."

PRO TIP

Take copyright laws seriously. Create visuals yourself or be sure to indicate whom to credit the photos or video to if an outside photographer supplied them. If a professional takes visuals but doesn't release full copyright to your organization, then you will probably need to check in with them and reference their name for attribution. More newsrooms are asking for written permission or signed agreements to use shared footage or video. Be ready to work with them on that, too.

PR WIRE RELEASE SERVICES

Tools can't replace humans in media outreach. Some pros like to use a wire service to send out press releases and claim those hits as "earned coverage." Rookies may even think they'll get reporters calling them after pushing a release through a wire. I've seen the opposite happen, especially with local news. Mainstream news outlet editors see something come through the wire. They put a mention in a brief section, and that's the end of the opportunity. A PR person can't go back and try to work on a more in-depth piece once that's happened because "it's already been covered."

Wire services need to be used strategically. The wire is helpful when you need to release information in a quick, uniform fashion. For example, financial institutions use wire services to release earning reports, and corporations may use them for nationwide product recalls.

In terms of strategy, you could suggest the use of a wire if a client wants to get information to a large trade audience or if they want to see their news online but there's no meaty angle to pitch. You can't make a molehill into a mountain through email pitching, but you can help with search engine optimization (SEO) and get some automated online hits using the wire. Some organizations are just fine with that.

Paid tools:

- Business Wire
- PR Newswire
- Global Newswire

Each has a different style, focus, and cost, so research them before use.

SOCIAL MEDIA MANAGEMENT TOOLS

There are over 2.6 billion search results in Google when you type in "top social media management tools." Why? Because managing social media channels is a chore! Saving time and scheduling content is helpful, so prepare to pay for some type of tool if you run an organization's channels.

Here are some tools that make managing *what* goes out on social media and *when* a bit easier. Most of them have free trials to test out.

Paid tools (their free versions won't get you far):

- Sprout Social
- Hootsuite
- Later
- Buffer

Free tool:

- "Schedule ahead" on Facebook

WRITING TOOLS

Being a creative, error-free, and compelling writer is a core competency of PR pros. Clarity is also important in everything you write. In PR, you'll be writing copy that goes into social media posts, press materials, websites, advertisements, and more. My writing has even been on billboards, wrapped vehicles, and sandcastles! Here are some tools that can help you become a better PR writer.

Free or low-cost tools:

- **AP Stylebook:** Purchase the online version annually at Apstylebook.com to stay current with Associated Press style rules and have access to a search bar. It's low cost and should be frequently referred to.
- **Grammarly:** An app that can be installed in most Google products to check for spelling, grammar, punctuation, clarity, engagement, and other mistakes. Free with paid upgrades available.
- **Thesaurus.com:** Look for other ways to say what you mean. Free to use.
- **AnswerthePublic.com:** Gives you content ideas. Find the most common search phrases on any topic so you can write about them and bump up your online relevance. Free to use.
- **A good human editor:** AI tools are great, but another human looking over important copy works best. Paid if you want a professional editor and free if you work together. Asking a colleague to lend "a second set of eyes" on writing is common.

FILE TRANSFER OR CLOUD STORAGE TOOLS

Sending high-resolution photos and videos takes more storage than most email services will allow. Use online transfer tools like WeTransfer or Hightail to transfer large files. When working with reporters, make and share a folder of visual assets, including logos, photos, and even video, using cloud storage options like Dropbox or Google Drive so it can be easily viewed and pulled from. Many times, upgrading to the paid version is worth the investment so your storage size isn't limited.

Free, upgradeable tools:

- WeTransfer
- Hightail
- Dropbox
- Google Drive

DESIGN TOOLS

Even if you don't plan on designing graphics as a PR pro, chances are you'll need to. Super-easy-to-use Canva is online and free (with paid upgrade options). Or go more advanced with Adobe Photoshop or InDesign if you're into creative design. If not, learn about basic design concepts so you can offer creative direction to professional graphic designers.

NOTE-TAKING TOOLS

Taking notes during meetings and important conversations is the sign of an attentive pro. Just like a waiter who doesn't write down an order and then goofs it up, not taking notes leads to something missing. Basic tools for taking notes are pen and paper. Laptops and phones step up the game with helpful apps or online tools. Typing out notes on Word or Google Docs can give you a running start on a recap. There are amazing digital tablets like Supernote that can turn your handwriting into typed words. I also like to use recording tools like Otter AI or Zoom to catch anything I may miss. Don't attend any meeting without a note-taking tool.

The toolkit you need comes together like putting together a makeup or travel bag. You'll find what you need in different places, but together they should work well.

CHAPTER 8 TAKEAWAYS

. . . .

To recap the essentials of this chapter, remember these main points and terms:

1. Having helpful tools in your PR toolkit will make tasks easier.
2. Find tools that serve your actual needs and are easy to use.
3. No one tool will do everything well. Pick the right tool for the job.

Important Terms:

- **Beat:** The subject matter area a journalist focuses on.
- **B-roll:** Recorded video of subjects or locations used to provide supplementary material for a film or television show.
- **Media list:** A contact list of journalists that can be created based on location or beat.
- **Media recap:** A compilation of media coverage clips and a summary of metrics provided after a media relations campaign.
- **Newshole:** The area of print journalism available for editorial stories.
- **Press kit:** Materials journalists use to gather story information (written in AP style).
- **Search engine optimization (SEO):** Ways to boost a website's ranking in search engine page results.
- **Wire services:** A press release feed used to distribute releases to the media.

PASS THE MIC 🎤:
STEPHEN MACIAS

For almost 20 years, Stephen Macias has created communication and PR strategies that connect brands to consumers in the LGBTQ community, communities of color, and female-driven initiatives. Macias founded the D&I practice at MWWPR in 2014, covering consumer lifestyle, diverse film and television projects, and nonprofits. He's worked with clients like Hilton Worldwide, Doritos, Amazon, FX, the San Francisco Gay Men's Chorus, and LA Pride. Macias has taken his work to one of the world's leading agencies, Rogers and Cowan/PMK, to continue navigating successful campaigns for global clients with innovative approaches to reaching diverse communities.

Q. What is the most valuable tool in your PR toolkit?

A. One of the tools I wish that I'd had in my own toolkit early on is the confidence that I've grown into over the years. The confidence to be proud about where I come from, be proud of who I am, and be proud of my family. That's one of the best tips I could share with up-and-coming professionals. As you move through your educational process or move into your chosen careers, make sure that your foundation and your children's foundation is based on confidence in who you are, where you come from, and where you are going. It'll impact everything you do.

CHAPTER 9

~~~

Think Like a Pro

*Who you are, what you do, and the life you
have comes from what you think.*

—Barbara Huson

Getting our mindset right for a career in PR is a
must for any long-standing professional. We give out a lot of
advice in this business and at times wear hats like "adviser" or
"counselor." To be a trustworthy guide, we first need to be a trustworthy *person*. That starts from within—with our own thoughts,
beliefs, and actions.

When I started my work in PR, I was advised to join several
professional trade associations to build my network. Organizations like PRSA, AMA, and the Hispanic Chamber have
enabled me to make business connections, find job leads, and
make lifelong friends. You'll definitely want to embrace building

and maintaining relationships in this profession, but be careful *who* you associate with. Some of the most charming people I've met turned out to be living shady lives. Like every part of life, if you're looking for trouble, you'll find it. And that's not what a PR pro should be looking for!

I've seen so much good and so much bad happen within and around this profession. I've heard tales of so-and-so offering special favors for coverage or so-and-so asking for a romantic date in exchange for promotions. There were workplace affairs, substance abuse, workplace harassment, and mental health episodes in between. It's not in my best interest to name names, so I won't. And it's not in *yours* to get involved in any bad doings or to spread gossip either. Too many people's lives come crashing down due to impulsive actions, bad choices, or negative associations.

A true PR pro should be mitigating issues, not causing them. Think of yourself as being called to a higher purpose as a PR practitioner. Strategic PR pros think about curating the career and life they want. We're held to a high standard of excellence. If you value your relationships in this career as the currency they are, you'll respect them and yourself in all situations. If you want an example of how *not* to be a straight-laced PR pro, watch the TV series *Scandal* or *Flack*. Those shows' PR pros may be good at cleaning up a client's mess, but their personal characters tarnish more with each tawdry situation. By the end, they're PR nightmares themselves.

Curating the right PR mindset can help us avoid scandals and perform better. In recent years, articles and podcasts have repeatedly covered the influence our mindset has on our success. Our **mindset** is how we view things in life. With PR, we should have a growth mindset first and foremost.

We never can seem to learn or grow enough in this business. To get into PR, you first had to learn about the profession, and hopefully that was through robust experiences in college.

If you were a student like me whose college didn't have a PR path, then you probably curated your own education model. Reading this book is a smart part of that effort! Which culture you align with or what environment you're in may also shape the way you look at the PR profession. It may have impacted the kind of education you've received about it. For instance, I had to persevere through college and find a job in the industry, all without realizing there were specializations to consider.

What I *should* know to work in PR seemed more complex because I am Hispanic. I've had to defend myself against an expectation that I should speak and write Spanish. A non-Latino counterpart was probably not asked as often if they spoke Spanish—or what was more commonly said: "You're bilingual, right?"

I always felt "less than" when those situations came up. Assuming I *should* know Spanish because of my surname or my looks isn't fair. In fact, it can be seen as a type of microaggression.

It's ironic because my parents didn't teach their children Spanish because they had been shamed for speaking it when they were growing up. I now know that was a microaggression. (Learning about DEI has been enlightening.) I've worked hard to prove my worth in this industry, and that means consuming as much education as possible that could help me in my career.

You may have reasons you feel less than in interviews or in the workplace, too. Working on cultivating a growth mindset means we accept our educational journey is never over. That's how a real pro thinks. We're never less than; in fact, having faced adversity can be an advantage. Few PR pros found their career by going down a linear, smooth path. How you started doesn't matter as much as where you go. Protect your personal brand by thinking about your career and your personal life as a tandem experience to be nurtured. Substance beats style in PR, and a strong work ethic, great follow-through, personal integrity, and a willingness to keep learning are attributes that are immensely valuable. Action creates confidence, and the more you do well in PR by acting in principled ways, the more confident you'll become. Work to keep your nose clean and your mind sharp. It'll pay off throughout your career.

TIMELESS PR PRINCIPLES

For almost a century, the Page Principles have proved helpful to guide PR pros' actions and behavior. The founders of the Arthur

W. Page Society compiled seven principles based on industry pioneer Arthur Page's lifetime of work and the tenets by which he practiced PR. Page was the first PR executive to serve as an officer and member of the board of directors of a major public corporation when he was Vice President of PR for AT&T from 1927 to 1946. Taking that seat at the leadership table as a PR pro changed the PR role from a task doer to a true strategic adviser.

Page's principles offer a poignant guide to how we should approach our work and activities. The steadiest and longest-standing of pros live by them. Here's my take on Page's principles:

1. **Tell the truth.** As communicators, we have the responsibility to be ethical and honest. Ensuring your organization is telling the truth means that we fact-check for accuracy before sharing information with a reporter or using it in content. It's about letting people know what's happening with good and honest intentions.

2. **Prove it with action.** Be prepared to prove any claim that's made. Or take actions to fix any wrongs before you talk about a claim. Public perception is determined mostly by actions, not words. Living up to principle one is impossible without taking the actions to prove you're telling the truth.

3. **Listen to stakeholders.** PR pros focus on building long-term relationships between an organization and

its stakeholders by getting to know those stakeholders well. Understanding what an organization's publics want, need, and value is key to sharing effective communication with them. Listening well means speaking with a diverse range of stakeholders using a tailored, inclusive approach.

4. **Manage for tomorrow.** PR pros should be able to anticipate public reaction based on what they've learned over time. Monitor the news to detect trends. Evaluate patterns in your community, and have the smart talk conversations needed to keep long-term relationships thriving. Work to create goodwill whenever possible.

5. **Conduct PR as if the whole organization depends on it.** Nothing should be implemented without considering its impact on stakeholders. Everything your organization and its employees do can help or harm the organization. PR pros should be at the forefront of encouraging good decision-making, policies, and operations that consider the diverse perspectives and values of the organization's stakeholders.

6. **Realize an enterprise's true character is expressed by people.** The strongest opinions people will have about any organization or endeavor—good or bad—are based on the words and deeds of its representatives. Every

employee is involved with PR, whether they realize it or not. The higher up a leader is, the more impact their actions and words will have on the perception of the organization. PR pros, especially those in corporate or internal communication, should advocate on behalf of employees so they, in turn, can be genuine ambassadors for the organization.

7. **Remain calm, patient, and good-humored.** Stay calm when things get chaotic. PR people shouldn't jump on every trend or follow a panicking crowd. When we face unknown territory, it's ideal to pause, do some research, consult with experts, and then move forward strategically. Professionals who consistently show discernment, are grounded in principles, and can provide levity are especially appreciated in uncertain times.

It's good to ground yourself in these principles early on. Life gets a little more dynamic and noisier by the day, and your job will get more hectic as you advance. You'll probably find the more things change, the more grounding these principles are.

PLAN FOR A CRISIS

Speaking of uncertainty, that's something PR pros have to get used to. Issues and crises pop up often in the workplace, and it's often our job to communicate about them. A PR pro can lead the way through all kinds of scenarios with effective communication. As a colleague of mine put it, an issue is like leaking gas. A crisis is like an explosion. Try to stop the small leak quickly before things get worse. First, consult with your leaders to determine the best way to stop the issues while causing the least amount of damage to the organization and its stakeholders. Then think through how best to communicate what's happened, how you addressed it, and future steps. Write that out in a short paragraph to be used as a statement if needed and broken up into talking points for spokespeople. **Crisis communication,** a strategic way to communicate during a threat to the reputation or well-being of an organization, is a discipline and specialty in its own right. Study up on it throughout your career. You will have the resources you need to productively deal with crises if you follow the PR principles, build relationships with senior PR pros who can advise you, and keep learning.

THINK CRITICALLY

Critical thinking skills are a must for PR practitioners. We need to be able to make logical and informed decisions. Knee-jerk reactions and impulsivity are liabilities for our organizations and for us. The saying "trust, but verify" is used a lot, but I recommend you verify, *then* trust.

I once had a boss who made me feel like a Debbie Downer whenever I questioned an idea. I was asked not to "rain on the parade" with my questioning. It wasn't my intention to kill the enthusiasm around a new idea. It felt like my duty to ask the hard questions so that we didn't run into a hard situation later. It's your duty, too. Don't accept everything you hear, read, see, or are told as the truth. It's beneficial to double-check, ask questions, and get things in writing (or document them yourself). Be curious and kind about it, but do your research. Discuss the "what if" scenarios, and fill in any blanks. Find what's relevant, and identify what's skewed by bias or opinion; then ensure any new situations are strategically stepped through. Asking questions like these can help:

- Where is the data coming from? Is that a trustworthy source?
- What seems to be the cause of this situation?
- What background information or context are we missing?
- How can we prove what we want to say?
- What are we missing?

Despite what someone may tell you, it's best that we think critically about situations. It's better for us to poke holes in things before stakeholders or reporters do.

BE A PROBLEM-SOLVER

At this point in my career, I can think of a workaround for the workaround in most scenarios. People love hacks and making work easier. Be creative and resourceful to solve problems. Find the solution, and present those options instead of problems to your boss or client. There's always more than one way to solve an issue. Staying current with PR trends, consuming the news, and having a network filled with sharp and trustworthy colleagues, mentors, and diverse communicators will help you find the answers you need throughout your career. Find a way to make things work, and people will appreciate you for it. There's always a way forward.

THINK PEOPLE-FIRST

So much of what we do is driven by serving people. If we have a people-first mentality, that will keep us from making mistakes that harm society and instead move us toward work that benefits our stakeholders. PR is classified as professional services, and it is definitely service-based work. All my first jobs that were rich in customer service experiences helped me become a better professional today. Anticipate what your boss needs, what your clients need, or how you can help a journalist write a top-notch story. Can you offer the TV station photojournalist a bottle of water at the press conference? Can you include food at your event that's being held over the lunch hour? What might people think when they read a certain social media post? How will your customers react to this proposed rate increase? Is it fair to do that right now?

Always look to build bridges and maintain the flow of information and resources across them. For example, when I worked in DEI programming, my inclusive communication approach to sensitive topics helped me navigate conversations better than DEI pros I knew who were polarizing in their approach. PR pros can help unite groups, and thinking of each person as important is the foundation for making those connections.

ETHICS AND CONFIDENTIALITY

You're going to hear and see some wild occurrences in this field. Not even because you're looking for it! People are fallible, and organizations are made up of people. I've been in conversations on how to deal with embezzlement, sexual harassment, domestic violence, alcohol abuse, and more. My firm creates crisis communication plans for clients, and each year these plans seem to get a bit longer. More and more scenarios pop up that could cause damage to an organization. At some point, you'll be called on to decide how to communicate about an awkward or emergency situation. When that happens, look to the PR principles, and remember that upholding ethics and confidentiality is imperative. Trustworthy professionals are strong in character and backbone.

When you're asked to keep something confidential, do so unless that puts someone in harm. Most of the time, confidentiality will be tied to an internal personnel issue, what a colleague shares with you, or what is not ready to be shared with a large audience. It may be tempting to share an inside scoop, but it's best not to. While people may seem to appreciate your intel, they'll also know you're not to be trusted with confidential information. Most of the time, the trail of blame will lead back to you. Waiting to release information (like an embargo) can be stressful, but leaking information will cause you much more distress. Don't believe in "off the record" because not all the people you'll work with may honor that. It's better to say things with intention and impact than to get yourself in trouble with a chatty mouth.

Don't do anything unethical to keep a job or make a dollar. Be a champion of positive change when things go wrong. Stakeholders can be forgiving when an organization admits fault and takes steps to fix issues. Remind your organizations of that.

Your personal, ethical boundaries will be tested at some point. Sometimes it's easier to make a change and leave an organization or environment when leaders won't do the right thing. I've been there, and it's not easy, but maintaining your integrity rarely is.

Always think like a pro and get out of bad situations (or organizations) as quickly as you can to ensure you maintain a stellar reputation. There are other jobs. Plus, freelancing in this field can be lucrative as long as you keep a strong network outside of your day job. You can always make more money, but rebuilding your personal brand can be much harder.

CHAPTER 9 TAKEAWAYS

To recap the essentials of this chapter, remember these main points and terms:

1. Embrace a growth mindset to keep learning and growing throughout your career.
2. Establishing your principles will set up boundaries and a way to simplify decision-making.
3. Think critically, solve problems, and plan for the unexpected.

Important Terms:

- **Crisis communication:** A specialized, strategic approach to communicating during a threat to the reputation or well-being of an organization.
- **Ethics:** Moral principles that can guide behavior in PR practice.
- **Mindset:** What you believe and how it impacts your interpretation of the world.

PASS THE MIC 🎤:
MARK MOHAMMADPOUR, APR

Mark Mohammadpour is the owner and Chief Wellness Officer at Chasing the Sun. After spending his PR career as an executive at Edelman and Weber Shandwick and after losing and keeping off 150 pounds over the last decade, Mark launched Chasing the Sun to empower PR professionals to prioritize their well-being so they can shine in the family room and the boardroom.

Q. How can aspiring or new pros prepare to healthfully manage the demands of a PR career?

A. College students and practitioners starting their PR careers should learn as much as possible about a job's working conditions and expectations before accepting an offer of employment. Health benefits such as free gym memberships and access to meditation applications only take people so far to address their well-being. We must have discussions around the use of vacation time, the impact of back-to-back video conference calls on our stress levels, expectations to be available on nights and weekends, and other boundaries to protect employee health.

CHAPTER 10

⌒

Act Like a Pro

LIKE MANY KIDS GROWING UP, I LOVED DISNEY MOVIES. Disney tells great stories. The movie that most stuck with me, and one I refer to often, doesn't have a princess in it. I talk a lot about Disney's animated film *Pinocchio*. In this story, the main character Pinocchio has a sidekick named Jiminy Cricket. Jiminy was an unsuspecting little insect chosen by the Blue Fairy to be the wooden puppet's conscience. He is appointed as Pinocchio's guide and is to help Pinocchio earn the privilege of becoming a "real" boy. Jiminy Cricket helps the now-alive puppet acclimate to his new body and understand the world he's in, and he starts teaching Pinocchio to understand the difference between right and wrong. Pinocchio becomes confident in his new abilities and starts acting like so many leaders do. They get swept up by the shiny new thing or the next charismatic person around. Pinocchio starts going down all the wrong paths and ends up a jackass (literally) that Jiminy follows into the belly of a whale while trying to save the mischievous hero.

Can you relate? If you can't yet, that probably means you haven't worked enough years in PR! As PR pros, we are often the guides for our clients or organizations. The best of us are the consciences of our organizations. That's why this career is so much more than just publicity or party planning. Real advisers are the Jiminy Crickets of their organizations. We're not order takers, and we shouldn't do anything and everything the boss says. PR can be a thankless role, and like Jiminy, we can be seen as the nagging do-gooder, pessimistic, and sometimes plain ole negative. I learned a long time ago that I should want to be respected at work and not worry about being liked. To be a true PR adviser, you have to get comfortable with that, too.

As the conscience of organizations, our advice is not always easy to take. The work PR people do is important, and the problems we solve before they even happen can't always be measured. We can't control everything that happens, but we can control how we react to situations, how we care for people, and the guidance we offer in good faith. In the end, Jiminy Cricket gets a gold badge for being a model conscience. Pinocchio learns it's better to listen to his conscience than to be a jackass. Like a small cricket, we can serve as guides from the most modest of positions, roles, or ranks. You *can* be an adviser. But first, you have to *act* like one.

MANAGE YOUR EMOTIONS

Impulsivity has no place in PR work. Real leadership starts from within, and managing how you react to external circumstances is an important discipline the best professionals practice. Our leaders, clients, direct reports, and journalist contacts will trust our word and guidance better if we behave like grounded, calm, and thoughtful individuals. Now that you're *thinking* like a PR professional, *acting* like one starts with controlling your emotions both in your professional and personal life. (Trust me, a messy personal life can damage your professional life.)

Our role is to calm chaotic storms in this profession. That's not easy, and it gets harder when people are tired or during periods of chronic stress. Learning and reading about stoicism has helped me center my thinking when times were tough. Stoicism is the philosophical practice on which Alcoholics Anonymous and Al-Anon built many teachings. It's very inner focused. Learning more about cultivating a reasoned mind has helped me focus on controlling my own emotions and reactions. Each morning, I read a daily message out of author Ryan Holiday's book *The Daily Stoic*. This helps me start the day with a resetting lesson and reminder to focus on what's within my control. Managing our emotions so they don't pull us in the wrong direction is conscious, disciplined work that we should pursue each day. Showing good discernment and control over your emotions will make you sought-out in a world full of raw, reactive people.

MANAGE YOUR RELATIONSHIPS

By now you know that PR people should be purposeful people. They must manage their relationships with the same amount of purpose. While we work hard to create relationships, not all of them should be maintained. There are times when we should apply the RPIE method to our relationships.

- **Research:** Whom do we need to connect with and why?
- **Planning:** How can we meet them? How can we bring value to that meeting so we can start a relationship?
- **Implementation:** How do we impactfully engage and create a mutually beneficial relationship?
- **Evaluation:** How's that relationship going? Should it continue?

The harsh reality is that as we advance in our careers, sometimes we have to end relationships that hold us back. That can be a bad workplace relationship, a bad work environment, bad clients, a bad agency, or even bad personal relationships. Business-wise, when people impede our growth, cause us unnecessary drama, or take without giving back, that can weigh us down. Countless studies show that women stop themselves from vying for promotions or recognition due to lack of self-confidence. Many times, the relationships women are in contribute to that lack. Work *is* personal, so *whom* you interact with outside of work or online can make an impression on *how* you are perceived at work.

Consider that, and make sure your relationships are supporting your career goals. In PR, how you curate, manage, and even end relationships can affect the kinds you will maintain professionally. On the flip side, bad professional relationships can hurt your personal ones. Maintaining the right mix and balance in relationships matters to your professional success and personal well-being.

MANAGE YOUR PERSONAL BRAND

How you portray yourself will form your **personal brand.** That brand is the image people have of you as a professional. PR people put a lot of time and effort into shaping their organization's brand or a top leader's personal brand. We need to put even *more* time into how we manage our own.

Our personal brands go everywhere with us and exist without us. They're impacted by everything we say and do, or *don't* say or do. Your brand is influenced by the verbal, nonverbal, online, and emotional expressions you share. Too often, PR people stay behind the scenes and sacrifice their own development to elevate others. Not managing our personal brands, which should be our largest assets, is a huge mistake. I've seen many pros neglect their own brands because they work for top-tier organizations. They think they don't have to network, join associations, or worry about career sites like LinkedIn because they work for a big company like Microsoft. Then they're let go or want to work somewhere else and realize their mistake. Pros who don't make the effort to have industry colleagues or personal brand recognition outside of their current workplace are in precarious positions. If people don't know you beyond your company affiliation, they can't refer or vouch for you when you need that help. Here are some of the most important tips I can share when it comes to curating your own brand:

1. Act Like You're on Stage

How would you prepare if you were giving a TED talk? Hopefully, you'd dress yourself up, practice your speech, and put on a confident performance. My confidence has grown as I've overcome some insane situations, and that's how confidence builds for most people. Confidence comes with action. Take action to make yourself comfortable in as many situations as possible, like performers do. Get out there, and get involved. Challenge yourself to get better at your skills. Be ready to seize any opportunity by looking and acting the part. If you act like you're on a stage, you'll behave like people are watching and like your missteps could be recorded. Taking yourself this seriously means you'll act in ways that benefit your personal brand. Advise your clients to think that way, and they'll be better off, too! Act like you're on stage whenever you're out in public. If you wouldn't say it into a microphone, don't say it (or type it) anywhere else. Remember that social media channels are a world stage, so always think before you post.

2. Take Your Career Seriously

Be sure that you take your career journey seriously and are your own advocate. Each opportunity, even seemingly terrible ones, can be a steppingstone to the next opportunity. Sometimes people start their careers or new roles without knowing where they're headed. Maybe that's how you're feeling right now. No matter how you start, getting workplace experience will help you sort out what you like or don't like. Sometimes, it's easier to figure out what you don't like! Use that understanding to move away from those disciplines or roles as you advance in your career. When you can take what you're passionate about and intersect that with PR, you'll find greater purpose in the work.

The most successful leaders I know use a proactive approach to managing their careers. They make brave moves and bold asks to advance. Get used to raising your own hand and asking others for career support, and be ready to offer it in turn.

3. Do the Hard Things

You're never done with education or educating yourself in PR. You can't possibly be *the best* writer, editor, strategist, photographer, or any other kind of pro. The field is constantly changing, so you have to commit to doing the hard things to stand out. The hard things are what others won't often do—like applying for industry awards, earning certifications, or learning a new skill. Maybe you want to work somewhere that requires a skill that's not on your resume. Go do the hard thing and get what you need instead of wishing you had. Writing this book for me has been incredibly hard. I've written most of these pages in the zaniest of ways to fit it into my already-busy life. Most of the words were dictated through talk-to-text while I walked the dog, worked out on the elliptical, or waited in line somewhere. Who writes a PR book while they're waiting to get on a Six Flags ride with their kids? Me! I accepted this challenge and found ways to make it work. It was difficult, but I felt called to share these lessons with you. I'm committed to doing the hard things that will help me ultimately help others.

As a PR adviser, you will have to do the hard things for yourself and for others. Like telling your organization to fix a process or facilitating some "real talk" conversations that can make positive change. Do the hard things, and you'll grow immensely through the challenges. Here are some *hard things* to put on your to-do list:

- Follow through on your commitments.
- Show up on time.
- Take and recap notes.
- Give back to your community.
- Give back to your industry.
- Make time for your family.
- Make time for yourself.
- Ask clarifying questions.
- Try not to ask the same question twice.
- Double-check your notes.
- Credit the source.
- Use compassionate communication.
- Invite others you respect to collaborate.
- Keep learning more.
- Share your experience with others.

Getting comfortable with things that are uncomfortable is the goal. Achieving that will take you to a higher level of professionalism—becoming a socially responsible pro.

PRO TIP

Social responsibility is now an obligation for organizations of all kinds.

PRACTICE SOCIAL RESPONSIBILITY

If you are unfamiliar with **corporate social responsibility (CSR),** you may not realize you are taking part in it when you participate in your organization's United Way campaign, recycle items in the office, or donate to a company-organized food drive.

The University of Texas McCombs School of Business defines CSR as the "need for businesses to be good corporate citizens. CSR involves going beyond the law's requirements in protecting the environment and contributing to social welfare. It is widely accepted as an obligation of modern business."

Recently, **social responsibility (SR)** as a universal practice has been elevated due to political and social movements. Let's be clear. You don't have to be a part of a corporation to be socially responsible. To me, SR is the effort any organization or individual makes to benefit their community or larger society through their work.

No matter how you define it, most definitions of SR include taking into account:

- Ethics
- Trust
- Responsibility
- Service
- Societal impact

Socially responsible professionals often act as moral guides for the betterment of others. As the conscience of your organization, here are four principles you can use to guide your organization toward SR.

1. Assess Your Position

First, consider your organization's mission, vision, and how it brands itself. Are you able to raise awareness around an issue that your organization has a proven track record of supporting? Has your organization shown a pattern of taking responsibility for missteps? Does your leadership positively encourage change— starting from within? Jumping into action to solve societal problems isn't wise if it isn't authentic or you can't really help.

2. Ask Tough Questions

Listening is the best starting point for assessing any situation. If you are tackling diversity and inclusion, talk with employees from different backgrounds, and ask for advice and constructive feedback. They will have the best viewpoints to help you understand what practices at your organization may need fixing. Companies can hire outside experts, but always work *with* your employees first to include their thoughts and talents in the process. The last thing you want is to make existing employees feel excluded.

3. Collaborate for Change

Social responsibility practices are a commitment to go beyond what's mandatory for an organization to operate. Working through ethical, economic, or legal responsibilities and ideals may take hosting regular meetings or listening tours with your stakeholders to structure an effective program. Sustainable changes can't be made overnight.

For example, before you tell the public how "diverse" your organization is, that reality needs to be a part of your culture and proven from within. Your employees are your biggest brand ambassadors, so if your diversity and inclusion efforts are only at a surface level, any external messaging will be hollow.

Social responsibility should not be left up to just one department or person in an organization. I've seen how even the smallest organizations tend to work in silos without considering including other department members. That's a recipe for blind spots and uneven program execution or support.

Ideally, a good SR plan should come from (or at least be championed by) top leadership and be shared down through all departments.

4. Be Thoughtful and Planful

Remember, what is helpful to society evolves with time. Always consider SR principles, but then apply methods against *what matters most now* since changing times can quickly change what society values or needs. For example, look how the pandemic made how we worked and lived shift so quickly.

Before 2020, many organizations shied away from sensitive topics. Employees now, especially younger recruits, are looking for organizations that are socially responsible and support efforts that benefit the environment, health, social justice, politics, gender equality, and more. Help your organization assess what really matters to them. Then either commit to helping in that space or don't step into it. Too many brands make tone-deaf or inauthentic declarations that are called out.

Planning ahead whenever you can and understanding what your stances are is critical to navigate the waters of social and digital media. Social responsibility done right by the community promotes the long-term success of an organization. This is a smart way to use PR for good and support the development of a better future.

For any practice to be authentic, meaning there's talk proven true by action, that practice should be integrated into all parts of an organization. I advise PR professionals to infuse SR actions into PR work as a way to reach the outcomes they are trying to achieve. What's wonderful is that being socially responsible should uphold the tenets of DEI as well. The illustration below is an evolution of my firm's PR and DEI Integration Model. It shows how together, PR and DEI principles align with SR principles. We're naturally in sync when PR is practiced for the betterment of society! That synergy can be powerful, and the outcomes of creating strong relationships and goodwill, mitigating issues, and increasing sustainability or positive societal impact are priceless.

Public Relations + Diversity, Equity, Inclusion + Social Responsibility Model

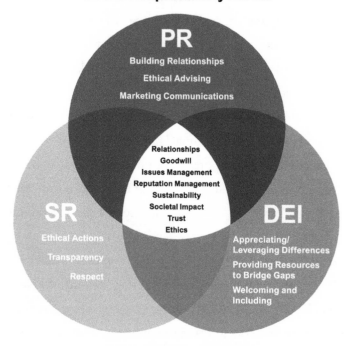

©2022 Melissa Vela-Williamson

THREE METHODS TO TACKLE SOCIAL RESPONSIBILITY

As individuals who want to be socially responsible, we have to be committed to keep learning about our industry. If we don't know better, we can't possibly do better. And real leaders know *and* do better. That's being socially responsible—not ignoring the role we each play as leaders at work, at home, and in our own lives. We can always do the right thing whether or not our employers do them. Approval may come from the top of an organization, but change can happen from the ground up.

Here are my top three methods for putting my SR principles into action as a PR pro.

1. Move Upstream to Fix Problems

Meeting people where they actually are is the best approach to connecting with them. Asking people to come to you for services or programs or to buy items just isn't as easy as bringing them your offerings. Moving **upstream** is a way to focus on finding the source of a problem so it can be fixed. The concept comes from moving toward the source of a river's current versus dealing with problems that flow downstream.

For example, going upstream in *healthcare* means figuring out what is causing a patient not to take their meds, which then lands them in the emergency room. Perhaps they have a mental health challenge, or maybe a lack of money is the actual issue. Addressing the root issue (like making sure the cost of the meds is covered) is a better way to solve their problem. For PR pros and communicators, going upstream to figure out the real challenges will help our organizations take the kind of actions that will make a lasting difference.

PR professionals have influence and therefore a responsibility to try to make their impact a positive one. To be different in the marketplace, keep from duplicating efforts, and really make an impact, go upstream from the social issues you want to alleviate. What could be the cause of this recurring problem? How can you help fix it?

2. Do More Good Than Harm

That doesn't sound groundbreaking or new, but so little about being socially responsible is. Ask this of your work: Am I doing more good than harm? Does my organization do more good than harm? There's nothing wrong with wanting to make money or working for a for-profit entity. However, making money in ways that leave collateral damage behind you is probably wrong.

Things aren't always clearly good or bad. Perhaps you'll work at a company where your service model must cause some harm to the environment. What can you do to make that negative outcome less over time? How can you convince leaders to improve things in the areas that align with SR and company values? Is there any way to counteract the bad with some good?

No matter your role, socially responsible individuals can help organizations do more good than harm.

3. Be an Ally

Even the best professionals have *some* level of **bias** (whether for/against something and conscious or unconscious). This leads us to a propensity to practice **otherism**—excluding an individual from a group we identify with because of their perceived differences. To be an ally, we have to unlearn and consciously manage our beliefs, thoughts, and actions. Whether it's racism, sexism, classism, colorism, or another "ism," I've found one thing to be true: We all have *privilege* in some situations and are *disadvantaged* in others.

For example, being a Latina has made me feel at an advantage in some circumstances and at a disadvantage in others. In San Antonio, where the majority of the population is Hispanic, it's not unusual to see a Latina in the workplace, and we're growing in leadership positions every day. When I'm at a Latina Leadership Institute event, being a Latina helps me "fit in" naturally, and being a part of that leadership program group is definitely a privilege. In the PR industry, being Latina gives me a unique perspective, and my work for the culture became a specialty. But many times, being Latina has also been limiting when I'm thought of as *only* being able to serve Latino audiences or accounts. This categorization ceiling happens to Spanish-language journalists, too.

Recognizing that we probably have some type of bias and that we've all been othered—made to feel excluded by something we can't control—helps build the foundation of how to be an ally. When we recognize that we also have privilege in certain areas, we can share that privilege as an ally with others at a disadvantage.

To be an ally, think about what the basics of being a friend are: showing up for people, taking risks to support others, setting realistic expectations for the relationship, making time for the other, and working through conflicts. These are cornerstones of being a good friend. My POV on allyship is based on those principles as well. Start by overriding your system—a brain imperfectly wired with biases—and think about how to befriend all types of people. Find something to connect on as humans, and try to support their positive efforts and accomplishments as you would a friend. There's enough business, opportunities, and customers to go around. We all have multiple identifiers (woman, business owner, parent, caregiver, dog mom) that we can use to connect with others. Our differences can be seen as limitations *or* as leverages. Let's think of them as leverage.

Anyone can work to become an ally. Speak up and give or share credit with someone who earned it, or sponsor a person or nonprofit that is doing great things but could use a boost. Invite someone who doesn't normally get invited to sit at your special event table, become a part of a leadership committee, or collaborate with you on a work project.

If you promote this concept in your workplace, allyship is a step toward showing you support SR because it's in alignment with diversity, equity, and inclusion. Remember, as an individual, you can do this yourself.

Consider me your ally. I hope everything you have learned from this book will give you an educational advantage you will share with others.

CHAPTER 10 TAKEAWAYS

To recap the essentials of this chapter, remember these main points and terms:

1. Act like a professional at all times to curate a favorable personal brand.
2. You can be socially responsible and produce social good through PR.
3. Anyone can be an ally. Work to befriend all types of people.

Important Terms:

- **Bias:** Prejudice for or against something or someone in an unfair way.
- **Corporate social responsibility (CSR):** The need for businesses to be good corporate citizens. CSR involves going beyond the law's requirements in protecting the environment and contributing to social welfare.
- **Otherism:** Exclusion of an individual because of perceived differences.
- **Personal brand:** The image people have of you as a professional.
- **Social responsibility (SR):** The effort an organization or individual makes to benefit their community or larger society through their work.
- **To be othered:** Made to feel excluded by something we can't control.
- **Upstream:** To focus on finding the source of a problem so it can be fixed versus dealing with problems that flow downstream.

PASS THE MIC 🎤:
KAREN SWIM, APR

Karen Swim, APR, is the founder of Words for Hire, a full-service PR and marketing agency that specializes in B2B, technology, and healthcare. Karen is also the president of Solo PR Pro, a membership organization for independent professionals in PR, communications, and related fields.

Q. What are some behaviors or traits PR pros should avoid to be successful in their careers?

A. PR professionals should avoid bias and rigidity. Our jobs require us to challenge perception to ensure that internal bias does not erode intended communication efforts. Unchecked biases can undermine our work and lead to a negative reaction from the publics we serve. We should be aware of bias in ourselves and organizations so we can ensure that we are broadening the lens by seeking out a diversity of viewpoints and experiences. Rigidity is the enemy of innovation. We must avoid being inflexible to growth and change. We do our best work when we are open to learning and challenging the status quo, even when we have created it. Avoiding these two traits will help you to be successful and satisfied in your work.

Conclusion

DID YOU READ THE ENTIRE BOOK? I'M SO PROUD OF YOU! Taking time to focus on our own professional development is hard. Being aware of our gaps and making moves to fill them is even harder.

You may feel overwhelmed by all you learned in these chapters. It can be scary to realize there's more to something than you thought. Remember, my stories, concepts, principles, and tools came from almost two decades of work in PR. You don't have to tackle all the concepts at once. Make this a guide you refer to as you go through your career. There are going to be so many times you're unsure of what you're doing, and I want this to be part of your long-term toolkit.

I ran into a friend the other day who I hadn't seen since she changed jobs. She transitioned from journalism into PR but had just shifted back to work in journalism. When I told her about whom I was writing my book for and why, she shook her head enthusiastically in agreement.

"Oh my gosh, yes! Journalists need this. When I was in PR, I felt like I was failing every day on the job! It's a whole different mindset I had to learn. I could have used a mentor early on."

I wish I could have provided this book to my friend as a guide before she started. I hope this book will help *you* feel more confident about working in PR. There's so much more I'd like to tell you about how to succeed in this industry. This book was a good start to get you going. To drive home all you learned, let's review the main takeaways:

1. Public relations involves more than just media relations.
2. Any adversity you have faced can be an advantage to you as a PR pro if you use it to connect with others.
3. It's important to build and maintain the kind of professional brand you want to be known for, even in your personal life.
4. Curating a portfolio of experience is a difference-maker for students but can also be done after you graduate or while you're working in another field.
5. Learning how to develop and implement a strategic PR plan will put you on a higher level than those who can't.
6. Building relationships to help you do your job and advance your career is vital.
7. You can have a PR POV, but you need to know enough

about the other communication disciplines to be a
strategic adviser.

8. Working with journalists is complex but rewarding.
   Becoming their source is the gold standard of
   media relations.

9. There are lots of tools that can help you do your job
   better. Find tools that you're comfortable with and
   ones that can make tasks easier to do and also easier
   to replicate.

10. You can connect with people by respecting their cultures and speaking to their values.

11. Having the right mindset is foundational for thinking
    like a PR pro.

12. There's a difference between knowing and doing.
    Act like a pro in and out of the workplace to be seen
    as trustworthy.

Remember, there's a place for you in PR. Society is made up
of all kinds of people, so we need all kinds of people practicing
PR. Now that you know how the profession really works, pay it
forward and invite someone along.

This book was a labor of love—my love for the profession
and my love for people. It is my legacy, leave-behind attempt to
pull back the curtain and share how PR works with anyone who
wants to learn about it. This book is the most scalable way I could

be the mentor and share the advice I wish I could share with each of you individually. You're going to learn so much through your own career journey. Find *your* way to share those lessons, too.

Remember, there isn't anything exclusionary about PR that prevents people from diverse backgrounds—or graduates who didn't formally study PR—from succeeding. Representation matters, and seeing or knowing someone we relate to can be inspirational to individuals from backgrounds that are similar. If you finished this book, you are ready to go make a difference in PR. Once you're on your way, invite and guide aspiring pros into the field. Invite the next generation of students without PR knowledge, especially students of color, into the field. Or share this book with journalists who are looking for a change. With everyone's help, we can shift the industry numbers to better reflect the communities we serve.

Many just aren't aware of the industry. Or they're not prepared to work in PR due to a lack of real-world experience. That ends with your help. Go run your own race, but keep passing the baton! I'm cheering you on.

Let's stay in touch! I'd be honored to be your resource and in your network. If you're overwhelmed, I can guide you with individual coaching or consultation. My firm, MVW Communications, serves clients who need help with strategic PR planning, DEI communication strategy, cultural strategy, PR, and other communication services. I'm available for speaking, training, and workshops on topics in this book and more. Connect with me at www.mvw360.com/connect.

There are links to the *Smart Talk Series* podcast, my blog, our MVW social media channels, and our online industry merchandise shop PR Pro Gear at mvw360.com. Take a photo with the book, tag MVW Communications, and share it on social to help us invite others into PR. We'll give it some online love right back. We're proud to elevate inspiring and generous pros just like you!

Acknowledgments

THERE ARE SO MANY PEOPLE WHO INSPIRED ME TO WRITE this book or supported me through the journey of bringing it to life. Thank you, thank you!

First, this book would not have been possible without the support of my best friend and husband, James. James, thank you for managing the house and kids when I had to leave for hours at a time to write or edit this book. I know it was a lot of work! I appreciate all the extra words of encouragement you gave me when I needed them and that you made space for another one of my big ideas.

Much love goes to my children Emilia and Logan, who make me want to be bolder, try harder, and leave behind a legacy that will inspire them to go after their own dreams. We can do hard things!

Thank you to my mother, who taught me the value of investing in my education, how to creatively solve problems, and what it means to persevere.

To my professional guides and mentors: Thank you to every employer I've had that let me practice the PR profession and to every experienced professional who shared guidance as I learned along the way.

To my clients who have trusted me and partnered with me through campaigns big and small: Thank you. Being able to learn what's special about your organizations, create new initiatives, or tell untold stories makes this work invaluable to me and the communities you serve.

Special thanks to all the professionals who let me interview them for "Pass the Mic" or other parts of this book. Sharing your perspectives added great value to each section of *Smart Talk*.

Big appreciation to my beta readers, Alexandra, Julia, and Catherine, for reading the manuscript and sharing your comments on what was helpful and what needed improvement.

Big thanks to my MVW Communications teammates, Maren, Mari, Julia, Jennifer, Jessica, Brittany, Ruben, and those who moonlight for us. You offered to lend an extra hand with work needs, eased my mind when I worried that I'd taken on too much, and cheered me on as I kept going.

Shoutout to my trade association mentors, fellow board members, colleagues, and friends at PRSA San Antonio, AMA San Antonio, PRSA Strategies & Tactics' editorial team, the PRCA of Americas, the Hispanic Public Relations Society of America Texas, and San Antonio Association of Hispanic Journalists. Your mentoring, professional education, platforms, and referrals have helped me professionally in every way possible.

Thank you to the Public Relations Society of America for allowing me to repurpose some of my 2021 column-writing copy for inclusion in the book—Copyright 2021. Reprinted with the permission of the Public Relations Society of America (www.prsa.org).

Finally, thank you to Lorenzo for telling me about Scribe Media and to my author/publishing team at Scribe for answering my questions, editing this manuscript in AP style, and meeting all our deadlines. We did it!